THEMES
for early years

AUTUMN & WINTER FESTIVALS

CAROLE COURT

Author Carole Court
Editor Jane Bishop
Assistant editor Sally Gray
Series designer Lynne Joesbury
Designer Claire Belcher
Illustrations Kim Woolley
Cover Lynne Joesbury
Action Rhymes, Poems and Stories compiled by Jackie Andrews
Songs compiled by Peter Morrell
Assemblies chapter by Lesley Prior

Designed using Adobe Pagemaker
Processed by Scholastic Ltd, Leamington Spa

Published by Scholastic Ltd, Villiers House, Clarendon Avenue, Leamington Spa, Warwickshire CV32 5PR

3 4 5 6 7 8 9 8 9 0 1 2 3 4 5 6

The publishers gratefully acknowledge permission to reproduce the following copyright material:
Jackie Andrews for 'The Chinese New Year Story' © 1997' 'Hanukkah - The Festival of Lights' © 1997, Jackie Andrews and 'The Story Of Divali' © 1997, Jackie Andrews; **Clive Barnwell** for 'Ready For The Harvest' © 1997 Clive Barnwell; **Sue Cowling** for 'Hanukkah' © 1997, Sue Cowling and 'Seaside Harvest' © 1977, Sue Cowling; **Margaret Eustace** for 'Grandpa's Day' © 1997, Margaret Eustace; **Aileen Fisher** for 'Light The Festive Candles' by Aileen Fisher fromSkip Around The Year © 1967 Aileen Fisher (1967, Thomas Y. Crowell, New York); **Lesley Funge** for 'Bonfire Night' © 1997 Lesley Funge; **John Foster** for 'Guru Nanak's Birthday' © 1997, John Foster; **Jean Gilbert** for 'Autumn Harvest' © 1997, Jean Gilbert; **Jean Kenward** for 'New Year' from Let's Celebrate © 1989, Jean Kenward (1989, O.U.P.); **Hazel Hobbs** for 'Christmas' and 'Chinese New Year' © 1997, Hazel Hobbs; **Jan Holdstock** for 'Harvest Round' and 'Santa's Sleigh' © 1977, Jan Holdstok; **Karen King** for 'The Harvest Festival © 1997, Karen King; **Wendy Larmont** for 'Divali Starts Today' © 1997, Wendy Larmont; **Wes Magee** for 'Harvest Time' © 1997, Wes Magee; 'On Bonfire Night' © 1997, Wes Magee; and 'It's Christmas Time!' from The Witch's Brew by Wes Magee © 1989, Wes Magee (1989, Cambridge University Press); **Tony Mitton** for 'Pancakes' © 1997, Tony Mitton and 'Carnival Time' © 1997, Tony Mitton; **Peter Morrell** for 'Welcome Divali' © 1977 Peter Morrell; **Judith Nicholls** for 'Christmas Eve' © 1988, Judith Nicholls; 'Succot' © 1997, Judith Nicholls; 'Fireworks' © 1997, Judith Nicholls and 'Divali' from Let's Celebrate © 1989, Judith Nicholls (1989, Oxford University Press); **Sue Nicholls** for 'Advent Calendar Song' © 1997, Sue Nicholls and 'Candle Light' © 1997, Sue Nicholls; **Jan Pollard** for 'Harvest Festival' © 1997, Jan Pollard; 'A New Baby At Christmas' © 1997, Jan Pollard; 'Chinese Lion Dance' © 1997, Jan Pollard and 'Carnival For Mardi Gras' © 1997, Jan Pollard; **Lesley Prior** for three assemblies © 1997, Lesley Prior; **Susheila Stone** for 'The Story of Divali - Festival of Lights' ©1997, Susheila Stone; **Geraldine Taylor** for 'Valentine Card' © 1996, Geraldine Taylor. Every effort has been made to trace copyright holders and the publishers apologise for any inadvertent omissions.

British Library Cataloguing-in-Publication Data A catalogue record for this book is available from the British Library;
ISBN 0-590-53682-6

CONTENTS

CHAPTER 7: DISPLAYS

CHAPTER 8: ASSEMBLIES

RESOURCES

ACTION RHYMES AND POEMS

SONGS

STORIES

ACTIVITY SHEETS

INTRODUCTION

Festivals is a topic that recurs throughout the year. This book starts at the beginning of the school year in September and gives suggestions for many festivals arising in the following six months. Exact dates have been given where possible but many vary. The ways of celebrating can also be extremely regional or individual, and even the spelling of the name of a festival can also have variations such as Divali, Diwali or Deepavali. There are times when 'Festivals' can be included in a theme such as 'Light' rather than concentrating on just one religion. Learning about festivals can be extremely enjoyable, at the same time providing an opportunity for children and adults to find out more. Always remember that, to a person of a particular faith a festival may have a religious significance and should be respected as such.

HARVEST

The date for harvest is determined by local conditions. In the UK it is generally in September / October. It is a time of giving thanks for the harvest and is one of the oldest of all festivals. The harvest of the sea and industrial 'harvests' are now included alongside the more traditional agricultural ones.

DIVALI

This festival which occurs in October / November, is celebrated by both Hindus and Sikhs. It is now a world-wide festival but it is seen as particularly important in the Gujerat district of India. The Hindu story of Divali tells of the banishment of Rama and Sita from their kingdom for fourteen years, their adventures and of their eventual return. It celebrates the triumph of good over evil.

Sikh people honour their sixth Guru, Hargobind, at this time. He had been imprisoned by the Mogul Emperor along with his followers and refused to be released without them. On his return to Amritsar he was welcomed with lights. Hindu and Sikh families celebrate in similar ways: homes and places of worship are decorated, clothes bought, gifts exchanged and relatives visited. Lights, especially divas, are a main feature of the decorations.

HANUKKAH

This eight-day Jewish festival commemorates the story of the Jews overcoming the Syrians and returning to their desecrated temple. There was only enough oil to keep their lamp alight for one day but, miraculously, it lasted for the eight days needed to obtain new supplies. During the celebrations one more candle is lit each night in memory of the miracle. It is also remembered in a special dreidel game. This festival of light is a joyous family occasion.

CHRISTMAS

The festival celebrates the birth of Jesus Christ and is recognised by Nativity plays, cribs and activities centred on the story as told in the Gospels. In addition, there are customs that are based on mid-winter festivities and others that came from Europe such as the Christmas tree and Yule log. As a festival it is now associated with gift giving, lights, cards, food and Father Christmas. It is celebrated in all countries with Christian traditions and it is a time for thinking of others and giving to charity.

CHINESE NEW YEAR

The festival lasts for fifteen days in January / February and is the most important time of the year for Chinese people. The exact date is determined by the new moon. The story tells of twelve animals having a race to settle an argument. By using trickery the rat won and so the first year was named after him. The following years were named after the others in the order in which they finished: rat, ox, tiger, hare, dragon, snake, horse, ram, monkey, cockerel, dog, pig. Traditionally people are thought to take on the characteristics of the animal associated with the year in which they were born. Before the celebrations, homes are cleaned and decorated. Street processions, fireworks and lion dancing are a particular feature.

ETHIOPIAN NEW YEAR

Rastafarians celebrate their New Year on September 11. Their calendar is divided into months named after the tribes of Israel. The festival is celebrated in family and community groups by eating, drumming, and dancing as well as talks and films about their faith. Their African heritage, especially Ethiopian, plays an important part.

SUKKOT / FEAST OF TABERNACLES

The Jewish festival beginning on September 28 both celebrates the harvest and commemorates the time when Jewish people were protected during their time in the wilderness when they made temporary shelters to have their meals and rest. During the celebrations temporary shelters might be built and the Torah is carried in procession around the Synagogue.

GRANDPARENTS' DAY

This is a new festival celebrated around the end of September and is an opportunity to recognise the part played by the grandparents in our communities. Children can offer their grandparents presents, entertain them, and thank them for their support.

BONFIRE NIGHT

Celebrations on November 5 include bonfires and fireworks with food such as sausages, parkin and toffee apples. These serve as a reminder of the attempt by a group of conspirators to blow up the Houses of Parliament in 1605. Guy Fawkes was caught and executed. Each year the Yeomen of the Guard still search the vaults prior to the State Opening of Parliament.

GURU NANAK'S BIRTHDAY

Although born in April, his birthday is celebrated on November 25 and it is one of the most important days in the Sikh year. Guru Nanak started the Sikh religion based on his belief that there is one God and that all people should work for the good of others. He travelled widely and introduced the idea of the free kitchen (langar).

NEW YEAR'S DAY

The Roman god Janus was thought to look both forwards and backwards. January 1 is a time to recall the events of the previous year and make resolutions for the new one. It is usually welcomed by parties and 'first footing'. It is particularly important in Scotland where it is known as Hogmanay and the song 'Auld Lang Syne' is associated with the festival.

ST. VALENTINE'S DAY

The festival now celebrated on February 14 dates back to Roman times when young people used to dance at the Spring festival of Lupercalia where traditionally they drew lots to determine their partners. In the third century Roman soldiers were forbidden to marry so that they would concentrate on fighting but Bishop Valentine refused to comply. He was imprisoned and put to death on February 14.

PANCAKE DAY / CARNIVAL

The date of Pancake Day is dependent on the date of Easter. It falls on the day before Ash Wednesday and the period of Lent. Traditionally, Christians fasted at this time as a reminder of Jesus fasting in the wilderness and overcoming temptations. Foods to be avoided were 'eaten up' on the day before and as many of these were likely to make you fat it was known as Fat Tuesday or Mardi Gras. Many communities developed their own customs with one of the most famous being Carnival which was taken from Europe to Central and Southern America.

HOW TO USE THIS BOOK

This book is one of a series of *Themes for early years* books written for early years educators. At this young age, children are full of questions and want to find out about things. This book aims to foster and encourage this enquiring attitude. Many adults are reluctant to introduce Festivals as they feel unsure about their own level of knowledge and they are concerned about causing offence in what can be a sensitive area.

Activities in this book provide the information you will need to undertake work on Festivals with confidence and a full section of resources is also included. The ideas can be used in a variety of ways to support both long and short periods of work and with a sensitive approach both adults and children can enjoy the topic.

TOPIC WEB

On pages 8 and 9 you will find a Topic Web that shows how the activities in the book will help to prepare for all the subjects in the National Curriculum and the Scottish 5–14 National Guidelines. It will assist in planning Festivals as part of an integrated curriculum and in allocating time to the subject. The pages can be photocopied to help with your planning.

THE ACTIVITY PAGES

Major festivals celebrated by children are explored in these chapters. Specific activities are outlined but these can be changed according to the resources you have available and the imagination of the children and adults using the book. Each activity has a discussion section in which there are suggested starting points for discussion which can be adapted according to the development of your children. There may also be some background information relevant to the activity. In some cases the children and adults can take pleasure in finding out new information about a festival together.

DISPLAYS

General advice on displaying children's work is included in this section. In addition suggestions for specific displays relating to four of the festivals covered in the previous chapters are described.

ASSEMBLIES

'Festivals' is a topic that lends itself to Assemblies and sharing times. This chapter gives specific ideas based on festivals covered in the book, which can be adapted to meet the resources and time available to your group.

RESOURCES SECTION

Stories, rhymes, poems and songs which have all been selected to relate directly to the festivals are included. They may be photocopied for your use. Several of the stories provide the background to activity pages.

PHOTOCOPIABLE ACTIVITY SHEETS

Eight sheets are provided which can either be used as part of an activity or as a back-up on their own. The level of adult support required to compile the sheets will depend on the individual children. Some sheets will benefit from discussion during the activity while others aim to encourage independent learning.

RECOMMENDED MATERIALS

Page 96 lists many useful books and resources. In addition, your local education authority might have resources available for loan or purchase and the local library can also be a useful resource. In both cases plan ahead and allow ample time as many people will want to use them during the same period.

EXPRESSIVE ARTS

ART

Observation painting	18
Peacock display	21
The star of David	27
Artist's impression	37
Cut paper work	44
Ethiopian New Year	51
Bonfire night	55
St Valentine's day	57

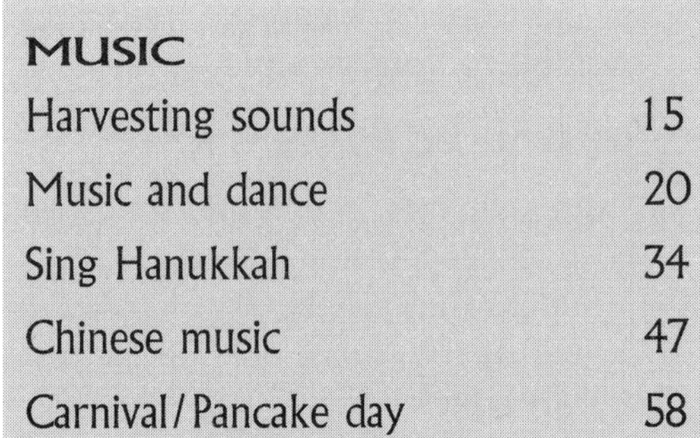

MUSIC

Harvesting sounds	15
Music and dance	20
Sing Hanukkah	34
Chinese music	47
Carnival/Pancake day	58

PE/DRAMA

Let's celebrate	31
Lion dance	43

ENGLISH

Party posters	22
Big book storytelling	25
Listen carefully	38
Running the race	45
New Year's day	56

RE/ RELIGIOUS AND MORAL EDUCATION

Sharing with others	13
Good and evil	26
The Christmas story	41
Guru Nanak's birthday	54

Planning towards the National Curriculum and the Scottish National guidelines 5-14

ENVIRONMENTAL
STUDIES

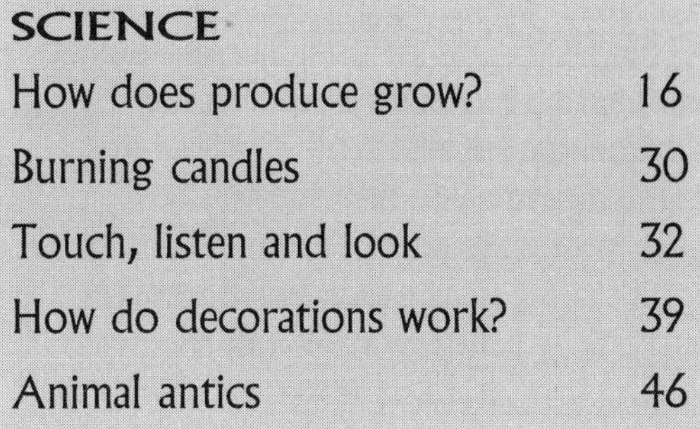

WINTER
VALS

PREPARING FOR PRIMARY SCHOOL

The National Curriculum was introduced to ensure that children between the ages of five and sixteen cover a similar curriculum in school wherever they live. The subjects included are Mathematics, Science, English, History, Geography, Information Technology, PE, Art, Design and Technology, Music and RE. There is a locally agreed syllabus for RE that will include aspects of Christianity, Buddhism, Islam, Judaism, Hinduism and Sikhism at different stages in a child's school career. Some of these will be at Key Stage 1. The local syllabus might also include a faith which is practised in the area such as Rastafarianism or Bahai.

TOWARDS LEVEL ONE

Children do not start on the National Curriculum until they are five. Before this age guidelines from the School Curriculum and Assessment Authority identify six Areas of Learning: Personal and Social Development, Language and Literacy, Mathematics, Knowledge and Understanding of the World, Creative Development and Physical Development.

In each activity children are required to enquire and discuss in small groups and often families and members of the community can be invited to take part since festivals are a community event.

THE SCOTTISH NATIONAL CURRICULUM GUIDELINES 5–14

In Scotland there are National Guidelines for schools on what should be taught to children between the ages of five and fourteen.

These National Guidelines are divided into six main curriculum areas: English Language, Mathematics, Environmental Studies, Expressive Arts, Religious and Moral Education, and Personal and Social Development.

Within these main areas further subjects are found, for example – Expressive Arts includes art and design, drama, music and PE. Strands are also identified within each subject, for example, Maths includes Problem-solving and enquiry and Shape, position and movement.

Most people working with pre-school children will find that they are already providing many of the experiences necessary to ensure a good foundation for the prescribed curriculum and the activities in this book have been written specifically to prepare for it.

The activities have been organised into separate subject areas which are set out in the Topic Web on pages 8 and 9 to help with planning. In addition to these curriculum links, Religious and Moral Education and Personal and Social Development are implicitly incorporated into most of the activities in this book.

CHAPTER 1
HARVESTS

Many faiths celebrate an annual harvest of produce, which provides an interesting opportunity to investigate making a model harvesting machine, to find out how foods grow and to paint some still life pictures.

HARVESTS AROUND THE WORLD

Objective

Geography – To raise awareness of the world outside the children's own experiences.

Group size

Small groups.

What you need

Some orange juice, chocolate, sugar, rice pudding, an orange, sugar cane, rice, a satellite picture or map of the world, selection of books and pictures which show how foods grow (available from libraries).

Preparation

Examine the books and select clear pictures.

What to do

Show the children the food items and ask them where they would expect to be able to buy the items. Trace the products back to their countries of origin. Use the books and pictures to find examples of the growing rice, orange trees, sugar cane and cocoa beans. Find the countries of origin on the maps for example, oranges – Spain, Israel; sugar – Jamaica; chocolate – Ghana, Brazil; rice – India, USA.

Ask the children which other countries they have experience of, either through visits they have made, relatives who live overseas or from watching television. Mark all of the countries mentioned on the map and indicate an import from that country if you know one. Some children might feel that they cannot make a contribution but if they watch television they are likely to know of Australia and America.

Tell the children to have a look at home for foods that use ingredients originating in different countries. Do they have any that contain rice, chocolate, sugar or oranges? Mark these products and their countries of origin on the map too.

Discussion

Talk about harvest celebrations in different countries and religions such as the 'Crop Over' parties in sugar-growing areas of Jamaica, the Jewish Shavuot in which thanks are given for the first fruits, the yam harvest celebrated with music and food in west Africa. Traditionally in Japan, none of the harvested rice was eaten before the ceremonial processions and dances. The Spring harvest is celebrated during the Holi (Hindu) and Baisakhi (Sikh) celebrations in India.

Follow-up activities

✧ Demonstrate the production of orange juice by squeezing some to obtain juice. Mix some juice with water and freeze it to show how ice lollies are produced from an ingredient that is grown thousands of miles away.
✧ Make a collection of food labels and highlight the countries of origin.
✧ Look at pictures of bread from around the world. Many countries have bread as the staple food but they are all different shapes and types.

HARVESTS IN THE PAST

Objective

History – To introduce the idea that things change over time by producing a group collage.

Group size

Whole group.

What you need

Pictures of historic and up-to-date scenes of harvesting, large sheet of paper, wide variety of fabrics and papers of different colours and textures, paints, scissors, adhesive, paper, card, small pieces of pasta, bottle tops and straws.

Preparation

Set out the materials for the children. Either enlist the children's help or ask parents to join you in preparing the background to a collage on your display board (include a farmhouse, fields (arable and pasture), narrow road, trees).

What to do

Look at the assortment of pictures you have gathered and pay particular attention to the features that are different to the present day. Compare the two sets of illustrations and invite the children to tell you what they can see.

Show the children the prepared background and explain that you are going to make a picture of harvesting in the past. Ask: what do they think we could add to it? Make a list of all the suggestions. Some of the ideas might be – wagon and horses, haystack, pitch fork, scythe and sickle.

Work with the children individually and in pairs to use the materials to make the ideas they have come up with. Assist them to get the size in proportion but let them take the lead in deciding which materials to use. The emphasis is on encouraging all the children to take part rather than on producing a perfect picture. Keep the construction fairly simple for example, paint a figure of a woman and add a fabric gathered skirt to give a 3D effect. Add sheep, cows and hens in the fields not being harvested and perhaps some birds and rabbits to complete the picture. Let the children make decisions about where features should be placed.

Discussion

Consider the pictures of harvests in the past. What do they notice? What would it feel like to be dressed like that? Can they see any evidence of electricity? What kinds of transport can they see? Can they imagine life without cars and televisions? Discuss the atmosphere at harvest time with all of the community being involved both in the work and in the Harvest Home celebrations afterwards. The last wagon would have been decorated and there would probably have been a large supper provided by the farmer's wife. The last piece of corn cut was traditionally made into a corn dolly.

Follow-up activities

✧ Visit a folk museum to look at old farming implements. Some museums have a loan service for educational use.
✧ Ask families and members of the community for any stories or photographs of harvest. Invite them to visit the children or prepare a display of their contributions.
✧ Make simple corn dollies from straws.

SHARING WITH OTHERS

Objective

Religious Education – To raise awareness of the idea of sharing with other people.

Group size

Whole group.

What you need

A copy of the story of The Little Red Hen (Traditional) with visual aids if possible such as pictures, finger puppets and magnet board figures. Large sheets of paper and thick felt-tipped pens, pencils, crayons, and drawing paper.

Preparation

Place the aids you have in the order in which they are needed. Have the large sheets of paper ready to record children's comments and the drawing materials on tables for easy access.

What to do

Tell the story to the children in an interesting and animated manner. In it a hen finds some grains of wheat in the farmyard and asks the other animals to prepare the ground and sow the seed. They all reply, individually, 'Not I'. She asks them to reap the crop, carry the grain to the mill, collect the flour, and bake some bread and again they all decline. Finally she asks if they would like to help her eat the bread, and the animals are all happy to help. The hen decides that, since she managed everything else by herself, she can do this too.

Re-tell the whole story with some of the children taking the parts of the main characters. Record the children's comments during the discussions, concentrating on those that particularly relate to sharing with others and helping without expecting a reward.

Ask the children to illustrate their suggestions by drawing, for example, a picture of someone they would like to share their toys with, helping to put toys away, taking flowers to a housebound relative. Add these pictures to the children's comments and display. This will form a reminder of the discussion about sharing and helping others.

Discussion

Why were the animals only willing to help at the end of the story? Was The Little Red Hen right to say 'No' or do the children think that she should let them share her food? Can the children think of occasions when someone has helped somebody else without material gain? Encourage the children to think of actions they can take – but only with people they know and with the consent of carers. How can they help the other people in their group or their family? Encourage an attitude that is caring but not patronising. What do the children have that they can share? Harvest time is a good opportunity for thinking about sharing – when thinking about the good things we have we can also think about sharing them with others.

Follow-up activities

✧ Make a collection of foods for Harvest Festival and give the produce to local people. Try to ensure that other local groups are not giving to the same people and that the produce given is suitable and useable. Follow this up with other contacts during the year.

✧ Visit a local mill to see how grain is made into flour or a bakery to see the flour being made into bread. Bread has long been central to harvest celebrations – particularly on Lammas Day (August 1) when a loaf made from the first grain harvested was taken to Church.

✧ Make a set of sequence cards to show the grain, wheat, flour and cake. Can the children put them in a logical order and tell the story?

CREATE A HARVESTING MACHINE

Objective

Design and Technology – To design and make a model machine for harvesting.

Group size

Whole group divided into teams of four.

What you need

Reclaimed modelling materials, adhesive, scissors, masking tape, paper, pencils, paint (optional), pictures of high and low tech harvesting machines (see local libraries for suitable books).

Preparation

Set out a variety of modelling materials. Introduce the activity by discussing the functions of machines using the illustrations you have found as a starting point.

What to do

Explain that you would like the children to be young engineers and that you need their help to design a new harvesting machine. Divide the group into teams of four, and ask two in each team to make the part that cuts the crop and the other two to make the 'gatherer'.

Ask each pair to 'design' their machine and explain how it works to the rest of their team and then to work in pairs to make the model. When the models are complete they can get together with the other pair in their team to join the two together. (Some adjustments might be necessary at this stage!) The completed models can be painted and finished.

Throughout the activity children may need adult assistance when making holes in card or in cutting some materials for example. Ensure that the emphasis is placed on the importance of the ideas and working well together rather than the final result.

Discussion

Talk about the functions of the machine and ideas for cutting and gathering. Which crop is being harvested? What materials do they have that might be useful? Discuss the suitability of materials. Will any of them bend, fold, cut or stick? Explain that adult engineers need to plan carefully. Talk about the children's ideas and encourage them to think of any modifications. When they are at the construction stage refer to their original suggestions. Give the children the opportunity to describe their constructions and their interpretations of the drawings.

Follow-up activities

✧ Prepare a display that includes the children's drawings and models plus their descriptions of plans, models and construction. These descriptions can be written by an adult using the children's own words.
✧ Add additional parts to the machines so that it can transport and store the produce.
✧ Let the children work in groups using construction kits to make a harvesting machine.
✧ Design a machine for a different kind of crop.

HARVESTING SOUNDS

Objective

Music – To produce a group composition to accompany the actions involved in harvesting.

Group size

Whole group.

What you need

An instrument for each child or materials to make home-made instruments such as boxes, elastic bands, tins, plastic bottles and dried peas.

What to do

Either hand out instruments to the children or make instruments with them using readily available materials such as an open box with elastic bands around it; an empty tin converted into a drum; a plastic bottle with a lid made into a shaker by adding some stones or dried peas.

Remind the children of the activities involved in harvesting – cutting, gathering, transporting, storing – and the type of action involved in each one. Concentrate on one action and talk about the sounds involved. Consider how to use the instruments to depict these sounds.

Make up a pattern of sounds together and repeat them to sound like a machine. Repeat the activity with sounds for the other aspects of harvest. With younger children sounds for cutting and gathering will be sufficient but later they can add transportation and storage. Divide the children into groups and put together a series of repeated sounds to represent a harvester. After several repeats slow down the 'machine' and turn off the engine!

Discussion

Talk about the sounds which can be made using the different instruments. How can we make them loud, quiet, quick and slow? How can it be varied? Discuss the movements of the machines and the actions involved. Talk about the different kinds of crops that might be harvested. Include different harvests such as a harvest of the sea or an industrial harvest. How are they the same yet different? How would the workers feel during the harvest? Explain that they work for long hours during dry weather. How would they feel when it is all harvested?

Follow-up activities

✧ Add actions to the instrument sounds.
✧ Sing songs about harvest time – see pages 75 and 76.
✧ Compose some music for the end of the harvest when everyone is tired but happy.
✧ Practise some simple barn dance steps to perform in a harvest dance.

HOW DOES PRODUCE GROW?

Objective

Science – To examine the growth of fruit and vegetables.

Group size

Four children.

What you need

Sequencing cards – see photocopiable page 88.

Preparation

Photocopy page 88 on to card if possible or on paper and stick on to card. Colour in the appropriate colours and cut out the cards along the lines indicated. For more durability laminate the sheet before cutting it out.

What to do

Mix each of the four sets of cards (trees, lettuce, tomato and wheat). Select one set and show the children how you decide to put them in order to depict the growth of an apple tree, a lettuce, some tomatoes or some wheat. Mix them up again and give one set to each child. Ask the children to rearrange the cards into the correct order of growth. Give each child the opportunity to try each set. Younger children may need to use fewer cards in their sequence to start with.

Discussion

Explain that the sequences show the pattern of growth in a very simple manner from a seed – plant – flower – fruit. Discuss the basic needs of light and water. How do other plants grow? For example rice or pineapples? What about some of their favourite foods? Where and how do baked beans and chips 'grow'? What foods do we get from wheat? Does sugar really come from a plant?

Follow-up activities

✧ Grow some mustard and cress and let all the children taste it.
✧ Grow the cress under different conditions (using varied growing medium, light, water, containers). Observe and discuss the differences.
✧ Grow plants from sprouting fruits and vegetables try pineapple, potatoes, onions or carrots.
✧ Try growing plants from fruit pips and seeds such as avocado, apple, orange, date. These may require additional heat.
✧ Name the main parts of a plant – seed, stem, root, leaf, flower.

WEIGHING FRUITS AND VEGETABLES

Objective

Mathematics – To estimate and compare produce, using simple measuring instruments and to use language to describe quantity.

Group size

Up to six at a time.

What you need

One kilo each of potatoes/ yam, cooking apples, pumpkin, spinach, satsumas and grapefruit. Scales, balance scales, chopping boards, 'mashers', knives, cooker or microwave, two saucepans or bowls suitable for use in the microwave.

Preparation

Get the area ready for cooking, make sure that the cooker is in a safe position. Ask the children to prepare to cook by wearing aprons and washing their hands. It might be helpful to peel the potatoes and apples ready for the children.

What to do

Weigh the potatoes and apples and record their weights with the children. Work together to prepare them for cooking, keeping the waste to a minimum and cook them until they are soft enough to mash. Let the children mash the foods, and when fully mashed reweigh and record the weights. Observe any changes caused by cooking.

While these foods are cooking estimate and then compare weights of the pumpkin, spinach, satsumas and grapefruit. Check the estimates by using the balance.

Discussion

Talk about the difference between quantity and weight. What changes in weight have taken place during cooking? Was it the cooking or peeling that caused the change? How could they avoid the differences made by peeling? What other fruit and vegetables are often bought by weight? Talk about occasions when they have been shopping and their produce was weighed. Have they ever helped to weigh it themselves at a supermarket? Talk about the traditional way in which costermongers (fruit and vegetable barrow sellers) celebrate the harvest. There is a celebration at St. Martin-in-the-Fields church (London) attended by the Pearly Kings and Queens who wear their full outfits and collect money for charity.

Follow-up activities

✧ Visit a market and look at the different methods of pricing foods for example: 5 for £1, 20p a kilo, 20p each, 30p a bunch, 60p a quarter or pre-packed – a punnet, a box or a net.
✧ Set up a shop or market stall. Include scales to weigh the produce.
✧ Make a photographic display of 'A kilo of ...'. Include photographs of foods that are both familiar and new to the children.

OBSERVATION PAINTING

Objective

Art – To observe and paint fruit and vegetables.

Group size

Whole group divided into small groups.

What you need

A selection of fruit and vegetables, a variety of wax and pencil crayons, chalks, charcoal, paints (thick and thin), paper of different sizes and colours.

Preparation

Prepare the tables ready for painting and place the painting materials close by. Provide protective clothing for the children to help themselves. For the first attempt choose a fruit which is a single colour rather than one like a mango that might be a mixture of colours. Arrange the produce so that all of the group can see it.

What to do

Look closely together at the fruit or vegetable which is to be painted. Examine the shape size and colour and decide which paper and medium to use.

Encourage the children to draw or paint the fruit or vegetable as accurately as possible. When they have achieved results with one painting, let them experiment with more than one piece of fruit or vegetable or using a different medium. Show the completed pictures as part of a harvest display.

Discussion

Discuss the shapes and colours of the produce. Notice that no two are alike. Even with two of the same variety they are still individual (just like people). Talk about the most suitable materials to use. What are the qualities of each of them? Do they want the brightness of thick paint or the pastel shades of chalk? Should the background paper be a contrast or the same colour but a different shade? Encourage the children to make their own decisions. Do all the children see the produce in the same way? Does it make a difference if the fruit or vegetables are viewed from a different angle? Can they suggest any different arrangements?

Follow-up activities

- Observe, discuss and reproduce the inside of fruits and vegetables.
- Ask the children to describe their own pictures and record their comments. Write these descriptions out neatly and display with the pictures.
- Display the children's work either on the wall or in a book format. Include a border of copies of other artist's work.
- Look at a selection of reproductions of famous still life paintings by Cézanne for example and discuss the colours and arrangements.

CHAPTER 2
DIVALI

The Festival of Lights is an annual celebration in both Hindu and Sikh communities which provides scope for activities from making puppets and peacocks to party invitations.

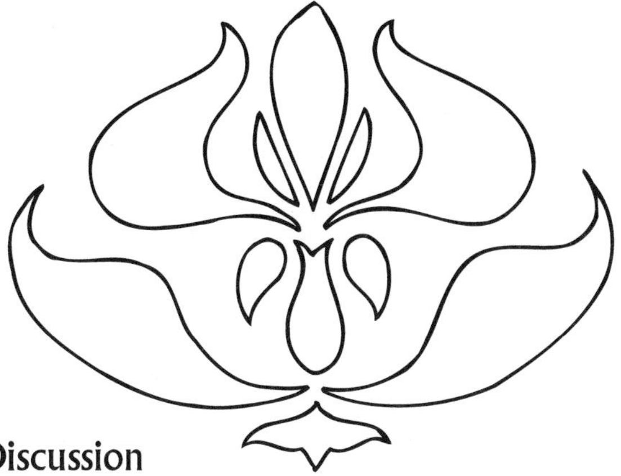

RANGOLI PATTERNS

Objective

Mathematics – To introduce the idea of symmetry through making a rangoli pattern.

Group size

Up to six.

What you need

Variety of coloured sticky-paper shapes, examples of rangoli patterns, scissors, adhesive, two pieces of contrasting paper approximately 20cm square per child.

Preparation

Fold one of the sheets into quarters, cut a curvy edge on the unfolded edge and open it out. Fold the contrasting sheet into quarters. Cut a design similar to the one illustrated on this page. Cut out the sticky-paper shapes. The variety of sizes, shapes and colours will depend on the age of the children. The amount of preparation required will depend on the cutting ability of the children, and many of the older children will be able to do some themselves.

What to do

Show the children examples of rangoli patterns – both commercially produced and handmade. Explain that they are going to make their own smaller versions. Ask them to look closely at the patterns and see if they can identify the symmetry. Show them how to stick the patterned shape paper on top of the square piece. Decorate with sticky-paper shapes, trying to keep to a symmetrical pattern, either by colour or shape.

Discussion

Throughout the activity talk about placing one piece opposite another, aiming to have the same colour and shape. Explain that these patterns are made to decorate homes and Mandirs (Hindu places of worship) as a welcome for visitors during Divali. They might be made of chalk, sand, flour or rice with freehand patterns generally being made by women. The designs might be geometric or based on flowers, fruit or trees. They can be rectangular, square or circular. When do the children decorate their homes? How do they do this? Do they ever have decorations outside their homes?

Follow-up activities

✧ Use the patterns to form a large wall display. The children can help to place them symmetrically. Ask the children to describe how they made their patterns and how the patterns are used traditionally. Use their responses as part of the title/heading of the display.
✧ Make symmetrical patterns using alternative techniques such as cut paper work, paper folding and tearing, blot painting, tie-dye.
✧ Make a large group rangoli pattern using coloured chalks. Place it near the entrance with a notice near to it that explains that it is a welcome to visitors.
✧ Place a small hand mirror along the axis of a completed pattern. What do the children notice? Does this happen along a different axis?
✧ Colour the rangoli patterns on photocopiable page 89 and use to create display borders or greetings cards.

MUSIC AND DANCE

Objective

Music – To enjoy singing a festival song.

Group size

Whole group

What you need

Pictures of Indian musical instruments such as the tabla or the sitar, or examples of the instruments themselves, example of Indian music (often available from libraries), copy of the song Welcome Divali on page 76. A cassette recorder. An illustrated copy of the hand gestures.

Preparation

Prepare the music, familiarise yourself with the tune and prepare an accompaniment if possible. Learn some of the hand gestures.

What to do

Look at either the pictures of the instruments or the instruments themselves and listen to music played by similar instruments. Show the children how to do some of the hand gestures associated with Indian music and dance. Practise together and encourage the children to try imitating some of the hand gestures themselves.

Listen to the Divali song and encourage the children to try and join in where possible. Older children could learn the words – perhaps in Gujerati if possible.

Ask the children to listen to the music again and this time to join in with gestures if they feel confident.

Discussion

Talk about the instruments. What do the children notice about them? Explain that music plays an important part in Indian life. There are regional differences but in all areas there is a wide variety of film, classical, folk and religious music. Have any of the children heard any Indian influence on popular music in this country? Although Divali is celebrated throughout India it is a particularly important festival in the Gujerat district. The Sikh story is especially celebrated in the Punjab where Panjabi is spoken.

Follow-up activities

✧ Stick dancing is popular at this time. Make sticks as an accompaniment to dance by cutting broomsticks (or similar) to approximately 30cm long. Paint and decorate them with patterns going around the stick. Attach a bell or tassel to one end of the stick. When dancing each child holds two sticks that are either hit together or with another dancer.

✧ Try some Gujerati or Panjabi writing such as Happy Divali (see page 22).

✧ Listen to different kinds of Indian music and consider the type of instruments needed.

PEACOCK DISPLAY

Objective

Art – To use shades of two colours to make a traditional design.

Group size

Whole group.

What you need

Large backing sheet, adhesive, scissors, fabric for the peacock's body, padding for the body such as foam pieces or cut-up pieces of old tights, paper or card 'feathers' for individual children, wide variety of blue and green collage materials such as fabric, shiny-paper, foil, glitter, glossy magazine paper, tissue paper, sweet papers and colouring materials. Picture of a peacock showing its feathers.

Preparation

Draw a large peacock body and head on to the backing paper. Cover it with the fabric and stuff it slightly to give a 3D effect. Prepare enough 'feathers' to give each child at least one and to make a large tail. For younger children cut the collage materials into small pieces.

What to do

Examine the reference picture of the peacock together and look at the colours of the peacock feathers. Explain that you would like the children to make feathers for your peacock's tail using blue and green on each one. Provide a choice of materials from the range available, and help the children to stick the materials to their feather shapes. When they are completed help the children to fix their feathers in place. Some of the feathers might benefit from fringing the top before sticking them in place.

Discussion

Explain that the peacock is used in traditional Indian designs. Describe the effect of the peacock raising its tail feathers. Have any of the children seen a live peacock? Talk about the colour combinations of blue and green. How can the children combine the two on their 'feathers'? Discuss the effects that can be produced by the different materials. Talk about other traditional designs and decorations that might be seen at Divali time such as the mango and lotus shapes and mehndi patterns on hands and feet.

Follow-up activities

✧ Make other decorations based on traditional designs such as the mango shape.
✧ Cut out some hand shapes and make mehndi patterns. These can be as simple or as complex as the children wish. The hand patterns are worn by Indian women and girls during many celebrations and, as they are made of henna, they last for several weeks. Many of the designs are based on the eye of the peacock or the mango shape.
✧ The Goddess Lakshmi is frequently associated with the lotus flower. Make a lotus design by cutting out separate petals and joining them at one point with a split pin. The petals can then be arranged.

PARTY POSTERS

Objective

English – To plan and prepare an invitation.

Group size

Up to 10 in a group.

What you need

Large sheet of paper for the poster, paper the same colour as the poster for illustrations and the recording of children's comments, scrap paper, pencils, scissors, felt-tipped pens or crayons, adhesive, thick felt-tipped pen in a distinctive colour.

Preparation

Cut the paper for illustrations.

What to do

Explain that together you are going to plan a party and that you need to make a poster to tell people about it and to invite them. Decide together when and where the party will be held. Think about the things you might do at the party. What kind of food will be needed? Is there anywhere locally that you can get Indian food, especially sweets such as barfi and jalebi that would traditionally be eaten at this time? How will you welcome your guests? Perhaps they could each have a garland and a Divali card? Would Indian music in the background help to create the right atmosphere?

Give the children pieces of paper each to illustrate the various activities while an adult writes up the children's decisions about the party on strips of matching paper. When these are completed involve the children in making decisions about the positioning of the writing and illustrations so as to give maximum effect. Where should they now place the invitation? Stick all of the pieces in place and encourage the children to show their work to carers when they are collected.

Discussion

Discuss the reasons for having the party and explain that Hindu and Sikh families celebrate at this time with family parties and community celebrations. Discuss the best venue for the party. Will it be easiest to hold it in their own regular meeting place? What about the time? Is it more convenient to hold it near the beginning or end of their session? Would one day be better than another? Talk about the positioning of the items on the poster. What is the most important part of the message? Should that be in larger lettering? Talk about where the poster should be placed and the importance of showing it to families.

Follow-up activities

✧ Send out individual invitations to carers and actually have a party.
✧ Make barfi or coconut balls.
✧ Make tissue paper garlands for guests.
✧ Make Divali cards with a traditional clay diva light on the front and perhaps 'Happy Divali' written in one of the Indian languages such as Hindi, Gujerati or Panjabi on the inside (see below). The diva can be decorated with geometric patterns.

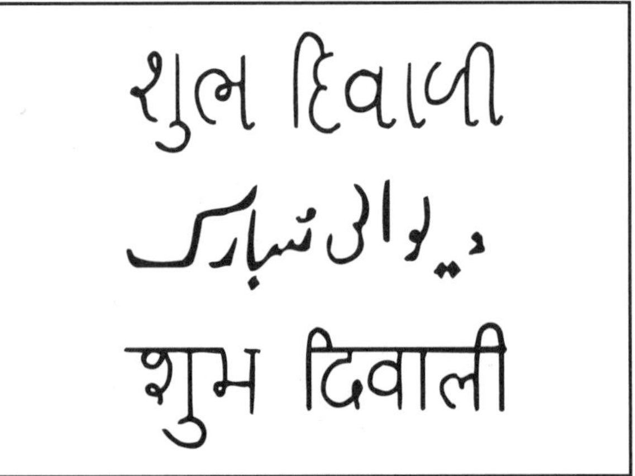

MAKE A PUPPET

Objective

Design and Technology – To make puppets of the characters in a traditional Hindu story.

Group size

Whole group divided into groups of five and six.

What you need

Each group will need: six small paper plates, one long and one short cane per child, string, brown fabric, card, paints (especially brown), masking tape, scraps of wool (especially black), assortment of fabric pieces for clothes, adhesive, small pieces of decorative materials such as braid, coloured foil, pieces of sticky paper (especially yellow).

Preparation

Have all of the materials within easy reach of the children and prepare the work surfaces ready for craft work. Tell the story of Rama and Sita (page82).

What to do

Decide which group will make each of the characters in the story: Rama; Sita; the King; Ravana; Hanuman; the monkey army and the people in the town. Make the puppets as follows:

Rama, Sita and the King – Make the face using a paper plate, wool, paint and sticky paper. Tie a short stick to a long one to form a cross for the arms (the children will probably need some assistance with the tying but let them choose how to position the sticks themselves). Attach the canes to the head. Choose fabric for clothes and cut to size (children might need assistance with cutting). Attach the fabric around the neck of the puppet. Add decorations suitable for the character.

Hanuman – As before but use brown fabric and add a tail.

Ravana – Cut nine circles of card and paint a face on each one. Add these around the edge of a paper plate and then continue as previously.

People and monkey army – Paint these figures on card. Cut them out and attach sticks to their backs. Add a piece of yellow sticky paper to a hand of each of the people to represent a diva.

Discussion

Talk about the characters in the story and the type of clothes they were likely to have worn. How can the children determine which puppet is the king? What kind of expression would the characters show? Who was kind? Who was angry? Explain that the story is often told using puppets. In some places, especially Indonesia, there are intricate shadow puppets and masks for each character.

Follow-up activities

✧ Rearrange the furniture to form a 'theatre' then re-tell the story with the children coming forward at the appropriate time.

✧ Encourage some of the children to take speaking parts in a puppet play.

✧ Make a wall display of the completed puppets. Add comments made by the children about the characters and how they were made.

MAKING DIVAS

Objective

Design andTechnology – To make divas (traditional clay lamps) using a variety of materials.

Group size

Up to six.

What you need

A selection of egg cartons, Plasticine, dough, clay, play dough, yoghurt cartons, bases of plastic bottles, cardboard, coloured tissue paper, a selection of materials to decorate the diva such as glitter, braid, sticky paper, adhesive, scissors, a decorated diva as a model or a picture of one.

Preparation

Cut out flame shapes from cardboard and use the thin strips of tissue paper to make flames.

What to do

Show the children how to use the selection of materials to make a basic diva shape. Look together at the patterns on the example you have (either an actual diva or a picture) and use the decorative materials as imaginatively as possible to complete the divas.

Stick a small piece of Plasticine in each diva and make the flames by sticking tissue paper to both sides of the cardboard flame shapes (make sure they go vertically to resemble real flames).

Discussion

Talk about the importance of lights in this festival. The word Divali (can also be Diwali or Deepavali) means 'a row or cluster of lights'. According to both the Hindu and Sikh stories divas were used to welcome people. Traditionally lamps are placed in windows and lit in the hope that Lakshmi, wife of Vishnu, will look in. She is thought to bring good luck – but only if the house is clean and tidy and all debts are paid.

Follow-up activities

✧ Clean the role-play area and decorate with divas.
✧ Make some 2D pictures of divas. Display them effectively in silhouette against a tissue paper background and placed in a window.
✧ Look for pictures of the Golden Temple at Amritsar which looks particularly spectacular at Divali time.

BIG BOOK STORYTELLING

Objective

English – To listen to and recall stories.

Group size

Whole group divided into two.

What you need

The Sikh and Hindu Divali stories (pages 84 and 82), pictures to illustrate the stories (try school's resource centre or a local library), paper and card ready to make two 'big books', flame coloured tissue and crêpe paper, paints, wool (any colours), thick felt-tipped pen.

Preparation

Make the books of different thicknesses – the Sikh story is far shorter. Punch holes on the long side of the Sikh book (to take woollen tassels) and stick a picture of a large diva on top of the other one.

What to do

Divide the children into two groups and work with one at a time. Have approximately twice as many children in one group as in the other. The activity for each group is the same but as the Sikh story shorter it will require fewer children.

For each group tell the selected story using the pictures to illustrate it. When you have finished reading ask the children, as a group, to re-tell the story while an adult records their version, in their own words. Help the children to decide which aspects of the story they will choose to illustrate. Let them make some large bold paintings. Stick these paintings into the 'big books' alongside a large print version of the children's text.

To complete the books add the title and decorate the cover. Do this by adding a flame to the Hindu story and woollen tassels to the Sikh one.

Share each 'big book' with the other group and make them available for children to look at later if they wish.

Discussion

Talk together about welcoming people back who have been away for a long time. In both stories people were welcomed by lights. How would the children choose to be welcomed? Explain that the stories are about people who are very important to followers of that faith. Have they heard of any other religious leaders or religious books? Hindus like to visit the Mandir during the celebrations. Can the children think of any special occasions when they might visit a place of worship? What do they do there? (Remove shoes, sing, be a bridesmaid.) Talk about ways in which the festival is celebrated. People of both faiths visit relatives, decorate houses, exchange cards and gifts.

Follow-up activities

✧ During the rescue of Sita, the monkeys built a bridge across to the island of Lanka. Try to design and make a long bridge using either reclaimed materials or construction toys.

✧ Act out the two stories.

✧ Ask individual children to re-tell the stories and record them in their own ways.

GOOD AND EVIL

Objective

Religious Education – To introduce the idea of good conquering evil.

Group size

Up to six.

What you need:

A copy of the story (page 82).

Preparation

Use the photocopiable page to tell the story to the children.

What to do

Explain that in the Divali story about Rama and Sita the rightful heir to the throne took his position eventually. Point out that this is an example of good triumphing over evil.

Describe a situation to the group in which it would be very easy for a child to be tempted. Make the storyline relevant to the group by adding detail relevant to local situations. Think of situations such as finding a purse containing money; accidentally kicking a ball through someone's window; seeing loose sweets in a shop and being tempted to steal. Ask the children to complete the story and discuss their suggestions.

Discussion

Talk about times when we want to do the right thing but find it difficult. Who can we ask to help us? Does it make a difference if we are being watched? Would it be better if we shared the money or sweets with a friend? What is the right thing to do in each situation?

Divali is the time of the Hindu New Year. It is a time to make a fresh start and to end quarrels. Talk about times when the children might have argued with someone and how we feel better when being friendly. Talk about strategies to have a happy group such as: we will share our toys, we will take turns and we will be kind to each other.

Follow-up activities

✧ Listen to stories from different religious traditions in which good overcomes evil such as Joseph and his brothers.

✧ Tell traditional stories with a similar theme such as Snow White.

✧ Visit a Hindu Mandir (place of worship) and ask Hindu people to tell you some ways in which they celebrate Divali.

CHAPTER 3 HANUKKAH

Everything needed to celebrate the Jewish festival of Hanukkah is included in this chapter to provide games, songs, stories and cooking for children to enjoy.

THE STAR OF DAVID

Objective

Art – To print the symbol of the star of David in a variety of ways.

Group size

Whole group divided into six smaller groups.

What you need

Selection of papers (various sizes, colours and textures), blue paint, blue 'wash', blue printing pad, potatoes, pencils, candle, wax crayons, cardboard cylinders, foam (suitable for cutting and printing), thick card, old toothbrushes, stencil shape of the star.

Preparation

Prepare templates and stencils of different sizes and from different textured paper. Cut star shapes from foam and stick these to cardboard tubes for foam printing. Cut a star shape on to halves of potatoes. Prepare work surfaces (splatter painting could be done outside). Ensure that the children's clothes are well protected.

What to do

Set different tables up for each activity and let the children try them in turn.

Demonstrate each process to each new group, or if possible have an adult helper at each table.

Wax printing – show the children how to draw a star shape on paper using a candle or wax crayon. It needs to be fairly thick and with the minimum of gaps. This can then be covered with a blue wash. Experiment using different colours for the star.

Foam printing – let the children gently press the sponge shape on to the printing pad and then roll the cardboard tube along their paper to give evenly spaced stars.

Potato printing – use the cut potatoes for random printing and then experiment with other patterns and shapes. Use different background colours and shapes to vary the effect.

Rubbing – make rubbings by placing paper over the cut-out shape and rubbing carefully with a wax crayon. Experiment with different textures for the shape for example, try corrugated or sand paper.

Stencil – use the stencil by holding it very still and drawing around the shape. Repeat around the edge of the background paper to form a border.

Splatter printing – attach a large star shape to a piece of paper and then splatter paint over the paper using an old toothbrush. Remove the template to reveal a star shape. Encourage the children to experiment by using two shades of blue.

Discussion

Explain that this symbol is very important to Jewish people. The origin is uncertain although it is known to have been used for several centuries. A blue star is now on the flag of Israel. Do the children have symbols that are important to them? Do they belong to any organisations that have symbols? The colour blue is frequently associated with Judaism. Do the children associate colours with particular people or objects for example a football team?

Follow-up activities

- Prepare a display to show all the different art techniques which the children have tried.
- Make Hanukkah cards based on the star of David.
- Print a whole sheet of stars and use for gift wrap.

COOKING POTATO LATKES

Objective

Design and Technology – To cook and taste potato latkes.

Group size

Six children working in pairs.

What you need

Six potatoes, two eggs, 50g self raising flour, salt, pepper, a little oil to fry, onion (optional), three graters, three bowls, three strainers, tablespoons, frying pan, cooking aprons, a copy of the Hanukkah story on page 81.

Preparation

Peel the potatoes and chop the onions ready for use. Prepare the work surface and make sure there is a safe place to fry the latkes. The children should wash their hands and wear clean cookery aprons.

What to do

Give each pair of children a bowl, a grater and a potato. Warn them about being very careful and to take care not to grate their fingers. Let them grate the potatoes and then place them in cold water while preparing the other ingredients. You can weigh out the flour and lightly beat the eggs and flour together; divide the mixture between the three bowls. Drain the liquid from the potatoes really well (it can be squeezed by hand) and then mix all the ingredients together. An adult should then heat the oil in the frying pan and drop the mixture into the pan a tablespoon at a time. Fry it gently and drain. Share and enjoy when cool enough to eat!

Discussion

Talk about the Hanukkah story (see page 81) and the significance of oil. Why do they think that Jewish people eat foods cooked in oil at this festival? What other foods can they think of that are cooked in oil? (Doughnuts, chips).

Follow-up activities

✧ Make star-shaped butter biscuits and decorate them with lines of icing to form a star of David.
✧ Have a Hanukkah party sharing latkes, biscuits and doughnuts. Invite the children's families to share the food. Make simple decorations and placemats.

LIGHT THE CANDLES

Objective

Mathematics – To practise one-to-one correspondence lighting one candle for one day.

Group size

Whole group.

What you need

A Hanukiah (the nine-branched candlestick, for details of suppliers see page 96 or contact a local RE Resource Centre), nine candles to fit the hanukiah, matches or a lighter, the Hanukkah story on page 81.

Preparation

Place the hanukiah in a place where it is safe but can be seen by all the children.

What to do

Remind the children of the Hanukkah story emphasising the eight days that it took to restore the Synagogue. Explain that this activity of lighting the candles will take place eight times. It might be possible for you to do it during the actual festival. Within Jewish families it would take place before the evening meal so perhaps before snack time, lunch or home time would be appropriate.

Ask the children to sit very quietly while an adult lights one candle. On the second day light two and so on. Use this as an opportunity to reinforce counting, add on one and match one-to-one. Divide the candles into two sets – those burning and those not. Will the sets be the same every day? Help the children to identify a pattern.

Discussion

Explain that in Jewish homes the candle would be alight for half an hour. Prayers would be said before lighting them. On each day children would receive a gift, usually money. It is a very special light that should not be 'used' in any way for work or reading. Discuss precautions that can be taken to ensure that candles are enjoyed safely.

Follow-up activities

✧ Make up a group prayer or poem of thanks. Talk about saying 'Thank you'. What would the children like to include in a group activity? Share the 'Thank you' with the other members of the group.
✧ Make a matching card game. Give eight children three cards each (approximately 5 x 8cm). Ask them to draw a child, a gift and a candle on three separate cards using bold colours. To play the game, place the cards face down on the table and let the children take turns to try to find a set of three cards.
✧ Use photocopiable page 90. Add a flame to reinforce the concept of one-to-one correspondence.
✧ Read the poem Hannukah on page 68 together.

BURNING CANDLES

Objective

Science – To observe and record the changes that occur to a candle once it is lit.

Group size

Whole group.

What you need

Large sheets of paper and felt-tipped pens for the graphs, four varieties of candles of different shapes and lengths and candle holders, ruler, paper.

Preparation

Set up the candles in a safe situation (where they can burn for 30 minutes in safety without being disturbed). Draw a simple graph for each candle.

What to do

Before you start, measure the lengths of the candles and write down what you have found. Sit the children around you in a circle and carefully light the candles. From their safe distance ask the children to observe what they can see happening. Ask them to describe what they see and record their responses. Explain that you are going to leave the candles alight until a particular time. What do they think will happen? Record their predictions. At the end of half an hour blow out the candles.

Measure the candles again and record their lengths on a graph. With adult support, older children may be able to use a ruler but with younger children measure out a piece of string to the length of the candle and use this to measure with against the ruler. Did any of the children's predictions come true? Repeat the activity until one of the candles burns down.

Discussion

Why do the children think that the candles burn at different rates? Discuss other changes that they notice. Encourage the use of descriptive language. Talk about the uses of candles – practical, decorative and symbolic. Discuss safety issues in the use of candles. What rules can the children suggest for their safe use? Talk about other materials that change as they are heated or cooled such as water, jelly or pastry.

Follow-up activities

✧ Light candles in different circumstances for example outside, in a jam jar, under a jam jar. What happens?
✧ Use the technique of observe, predict, observe with other scientific activities, such as adding cooking oil to water, putting celery into coloured water.
✧ Use this experiment and what the children have observed to explain how candles were once used as a way of telling the time.

LET'S CELEBRATE

Objective

Drama – To dramatise the story of a family celebrating Hanukkah.

Group size

Small group.

What you need

Pieces of paper and crayons, candles, a large candle, dusters, brushes, decorations, latkes, doughnuts, dreidel, dreidel board games (page 33), hanukiah, gift-wrapped money.

Preparation

Arrange your room to provide plenty of space for the children to move around and act. Place all of the materials within easy reach.

What to do

Explain to the children that you would like them to act the story of a family celebrating Hanukkah at home. Tell them that as you tell the story you would like them to act out the directions. In the last scene they will all take specific roles but they will start together.

Scene 1: Buy cards well in advance to send to friends and relatives here and in Israel. Make cards with a star of David decoration. Buy candles – remembering to buy the larger 'servant' candle.

Scene 2: Clean the house thoroughly. Put up decorations that have been made at school such as a stained glass window star, cards, printed decorations.

Scene 3: Prepare for the last night of the festival. All eight candles will be used. Make latkes and doughnuts.

Scene 4: Uncle, Aunt and cousins arrive. They bring gifts of money for the children. Uncle tells the story of Hanukkah. It makes him both happy and sad. Happy because he remembers how God looks after them all but sad when he remembers how people have suffered. This though is a happy occasion and they must enjoy the evening. The older children play the dreidel game and the younger ones play a simpler version that Dad has made for them. The candles are lit and Dad says a special prayer. He puts them in the window. Everyone eats, drinks and sings some favourite Hanukkah songs.

Discussion

Talk about the Hanukkah story. Explain that the Synagogue is very important to Jewish people so they were very upset when it was ransacked. Do the children have any places that are special to them? Do any of them visit places of worship? Are these places treated with care and respect? However, Hanukkah is a happy festival of light with the eight candles as a reminder of the time it took to restore the Synagogue. The dreidel game is also a reminder of that occasion as is the selection of food cooked in oil.

Follow-up activities

✧ Make cards and decorations for the group's room.
✧ Make group pictures to represent the four scenes of the story.
✧ Prepare the story for a 'production' by making more props and practising on a few occasions – don't take away the spontaneity and originality of the children.
✧ Make potato latkes with the children, see instructions on page 28.
✧ Look at a picture of the inside of a Synagogue and talk about its features.

TOUCH, LISTEN AND LOOK

Objective

Science – To use the senses of touch, hearing and sight to examine the materials and to make a hanukiah.

Group size

Up to six children.

What you need

A collection of hanukiah using a variety of materials and of different shapes and sizes (the activity can take place with one but will be more effective if several can be examined). Many schools now have them in their RE artefact collections or they might be available from a teacher's centre, RE collection, multi-cultural centre or library or a Jewish family. Pictures of hanukiah, cards to record general observations, three sheets of paper.

Preparation

Collect together some hanukiah. Prepare a free-standing card to accompany each hanukiah. Write 'We found out ...' at the top of each one. Label the three sheets of paper with these headings, on one 'We can see' on the second 'We can hear' and on the third 'We can feel'. Decorate them with brown and blue eyes, ears and hands in different skin tones.

What to do

Ask the children to wash their hands before handling religious artefacts and explain that they must all be treated with respect. Give all the children the opportunity to handle the hanukiah and to ask questions. Consider the materials which have been used to make them, methods of construction, ways to make it stable, how best to store them and the ease of holding the candles. Record the children's observations and suggestions on the cards, adding all the relevant comments from other groups of children.

Use the senses to examine the exhibits. Record these observations on the appropriate separate sheets of paper. Look at the pictures of hanukiah. Using the knowledge gained from the real objects, what can the children determine about these?

Discussion

Discuss the children's own observations and encourage them to ask questions. Do they think the material is suitable for inside, outside, or both? How long will it last? Will it break easily? Will it show fingermarks? Talk about showing respect for religious materials. Explain that it is important for Jewish people and reminds them of an important time when God helped them. Do they have any artefacts or pictures in their homes that have a religious significance? Talk about the importance of the hanukiah in festival celebrations. Explain that one candle is lit on the first of the eight nights. An additional candle is lit each night. They are all lit from the one 'servant' candle known as the shammash. What do they notice about this candle? (It is always different to the others and it might be at the end or in the middle.)

Follow-up activities

✧ Make models of a hanukiah using different techniques for example try salt dough, reclaimed materials sprayed with silver or gold, paper chains.
✧ Use the hanukiah as the subject of a greeting card. Place hands side-by-side on a piece of paper with a small gap between them. Draw round the fingers to form the candle sticks. Add a central 'servant' candle and fingerprint flames.
✧ Make a group hanukiah using a stained glass window technique. Examples of these can be found in many Synagogues.

DREIDEL GAME

Objective

Mathematics – To practise mathematical skills through playing a version of the traditional dreidel game.

Group size

Four children.

What you need

Four counters each of a different colour, four base boards (see photocopiable page 91), a spinner made from stiff card and a cocktail stick / pencil (known as a dreidel).

Preparation

Base board – complete each box by adding a colour, shape or number. Choose one that is relevant to the group of children playing the game.
Spinner or ' dreidel' – mark the spinner to match the base board.

What to do

Show the children the dreidel and explain that it is used by Jewish people when playing a game. Explain that they will be able to play it when they are older but they are now going to learn a simpler version.

Explain the instructions for playing the game emphasising that the emphasis is not on winning but playing together.

To play the game each child places a counter on the start. They then take it in turns to spin the disc and place a counter on the matching shape. When a child has covered all four they move them to the menorah. The winner is the first child to reach the menorah having collected all the stages on the way.

Discussion

Talk about the dreidel game reminding Jewish people of something that happened a very long time ago. Remind them of the story on page 81 and explain that Jewish people were not allowed to read their Holy Writing but they could play the game. Explain that the menorah is also very special and the eight candles are a reminder of the eight days it took to restore the Synagogue. The writing on a dreidel is in Hebrew. Talk about the fact that Jewish people live in many countries of the world. Wherever they are they will still have an understanding of Hebrew. What languages do the children know? Talk about taking turns and going first, second, third, fourth. Why do we take turns when playing games? Place the emphasis on playing together rather than on who wins or loses.

Follow-up activities

✧ Each child could make a game and take it home to play with their families and friends.
✧ Show the children a dreidel (or a picture of one) that would be used in Jewish homes. Older children can make one of their own.
✧ Make a collection of writing in different languages. Look, for example, on biscuit wrappings, electrical instructions, clothes' labels. Display and label them with the name of the language and the name of the country / countries where it is spoken.

SING HANUKKAH

Objective

Music – To enjoy singing together and providing a percussion accompaniment.

Group size

Whole group.

What you need

A copy of the song Candle Light on page 77, tape recorder, a musical instrument to accompany, percussion instruments (these can be made by the children), eight cardboard candles.

Preparation

Record yourself or a willing colleague singing the song with a musical instrument accompaniment.

What to do

Play the recording to the children and tap out the rhythm quietly. Divide the group into two and ask them to accompany alternate lines. Introduce the words to the song and repeat these as many times as necessary until the children are familiar with them. Some children might be happier if they just join in with the counting and they will increase their involvement as their confidence grows.

Gradually introduce the instruments. Encourage the children to keep to the rhythm and not let any instrument dominate. When chanting ask the group to follow your hand movements for fast, slow and stop. An action to denote quietly such as lowering your hand with the palm facing down would also be useful. When they are fairly sure of the song introduce the cardboard candles. Hold up one as each verse is sung until there are eight.

Discussion

Remind the children of the Hanukkah story and the significance of the eight candles. Explain that a song similar to this would be sung each night as one more candle is added. When Jewish people sing their traditional songs they are reminded that they are part of a world-wide group. Do any of the children have friends or members of their families living in other countries or even in other parts of Britain? How do they remember them and remain in contact with them?

Follow-up activities

✧ Listen to some Jewish music – Handel's overture to 'Judas Maccabeus' is particularly relevant. Traditional music is often available on loan from public libraries.
✧ Perform the song, with accompaniment and candles, to other groups of children or to families.
✧ As an alternative to candles make eight headbands and decorate them to resemble flames. As the song is sung, first one child stands up, then two and so on until all eight are standing.
✧ Record the children's performance so that they can hear it for themselves.
✧ Let some of the children be the 'conductor' using hand signals for quietly, loudly and stop.

CHAPTER 4
CHRISTMAS

Practical ideas to celebrate Christmas provide opportunities for number recognition in making an Advent calendar, technology in making Christmas decorations and recording and story-telling.

CHRISTMAS PATTERNS

Objective

Mathematics – To examine repeating patterns using shapes related to Christmas.

Group size

Up to six children.

What you need

Coloured blocks or beads, potatoes, knife, strips of yellow paper approximately 12 x 35cm (the size will vary according to the size of the repeat and the number of repeats), print pads with red and green paint, tables suitable for painting on, protective aprons or old shirts for the children.

Preparation

Let the children practise simple repeating patterns using blocks or beads. Cover your work surfaces ready for painting and set out the materials. Cut the potatoes into simple Christmas shapes such as a star, candle or stocking – make two of each shape (use sponges instead of potatoes if preferred). Prepare the print pads by moistening them with red and green paint. Help the children put on their aprons.

What to do

Let the children each choose one shape and print with it along the left hand side of a strip of paper. They can then select the same shape with the other colour and print next to the first colour. Repeat with the first colour and continue using red and green alternately.

On a new strip of paper let them experiment with using one colour but two different shapes. Allow children to continue experimenting with more complicated patterns if they are keen to do so.

Discussion

Talk about the shapes used. Why do we use them at Christmas? How do they relate to the Christmas story? What other shapes could we have used? Suggest a Christmas tree (a custom which came from Germany during the nineteenth century), stockings (referring to a story about St. Nicholas giving an anonymous gift to a family by throwing gold coins through the window. The coins are said to have landed in the girls' stockings), crackers (originated by Tom Smith who took ideas from French bon-bons, Chinese fortune cookies and the crackling of the fire), poinsettia (named after the man who took the plant from Mexico to the USA – Joel Poinsett), candles (symbolising Christ being the 'Light of the world'), star (a reminder of the star over Bethlehem). How could they vary their patterns? Could they mix the colours and shapes in a different way? What other materials could they use?

Follow-up activities

✧ Use the completed strips to make party hats, table decorations or a wall display.
✧ Look at Christmas wrapping paper and examine the repeated patterns used.
✧ Prepare smaller versions of the designs and use in a border for a Christmas card or party place-mat.
✧ Complete the patterns on photocopiable page 92.

ST NICHOLAS LETTERS

Objective

Design and Technology – To make and enjoy St. Nicholas biscuits.

Group size

Up to six children.

What you need

Aprons, clean work space, oven cloth/gloves, rolling pins, flour for rolling, oven wire rack, small bowl, fork, pastry brush, 400g frozen pastry, 200g marzipan, ½ cup milk, an egg, greased baking sheet.

Preparation

Thaw the pastry and heat the oven to 220°c/gas mark 7. Prepare the work area to ensure it is hygienic and safe. Remind the children of safety rules for example, not to touch the oven or things which have just come out of the oven.

What to do

Show the children how to roll out the pastry thinly and then cut it into strips of approximately 4 x 10cm. Then roll the marzipan into 'worms' of approximately 1cm wide and cut it into strips slightly shorter than the pastry pieces. Place the marzipan on the pastry and roll them up together and seal the edges and the ends with milk. The children can then form the strip into the shape of a letter, choosing their own initial or another letter of their choice. If they need to make a join show them how to seal it with milk.

Place the letters on a greased baking sheet and tell the children to leave enough space between them. Brush the tops with beaten egg or milk and bake them for approximately 15 minutes. Let the children help you clear away and wash up. When the letters are cool enjoy tasting and sharing them together.

Discussion

Explain that 'letterblanket' are frequently eaten in the Netherlands on St. Nicholas' Day (December 6). Explain that St. Nicholas is another name for Father Christmas (as is Santa Claus) and that he was a Bishop who became the Patron Saint of children. According to legend he heard of three sisters whose father was very poor, he climbed on to their roof and dropped gold coins into their bedroom. The next morning they woke up to find the gold in their stockings. The image of Father Christmas in his red cloak originated in the United States of America.

Follow-up activities

- ✧ Make a large class 'letterblanket' to share.
- ✧ Try other Christmas recipes such as shortbread or shaped biscuits.
- ✧ Talk about other foods eaten at Christmas such as mince pies, Christmas pudding and cake. Find out what traditional foods are eaten in different parts of the world.
- ✧ Involve parents in exchanging favourite Christmas recipes and perhaps even preparing a simple group Christmas cookery book.
- ✧ Make salt-dough food for the home corner.

ARTIST'S IMPRESSION

Objective

Art – To examine art from different periods and cultures and to use art materials to make a copy of a picture.

Group size

Up to six children.

What you need

Pictures of the Nativity, examples of art from different periods and cultures (look at Christmas cards and art books), books with Christmas stories from other countries, plastic bags/sheeting, crayons, paint brushes, different types of paper and felt-tipped pens.

Preparation

Plan possible questions to ask about the pictures. Cover pictures with plastic (opened-out bags or sheeting) fixed with sticky tape to protect them from art materials.

What to do

Show the children one-by-one the pictures which you have gathered from a variety of sources. Explain that, although the pictures are all different, they all depict the same story. Look first for the common features and characters. Who can they recognise in the pictures? Remind them of the Nativity story and see which pictures relate to different parts of it. Now see which parts they can identify as different? Encourage them to observe features such as the appearance of faces, types of clothes, halos, animals and stars.

Ask the children to each choose a picture, observe it, and then to produce their own version in a similar style. Show them the materials you have ready for use and encourage them to have a go at their own picture. Emphasise the colours and characters rather than a 'perfect' reproduction. When they are complete, make a display of the children's work together with the original pictures.

Discussion

Compare the way people dressed in the pictures with present day clothes. Why do the children think that there are differences in the pictures if the story is the same? Is there a difference if the picture comes from a hot country? Do any of the pictures give any indication of how Christmas is celebrated in another country?

Follow-up activities

✧ Make a collection of old Christmas cards showing Christmas in the past. Either display them or make a group scrapbook. How do we know that they are in the past?
✧ Find out about Christmas in other countries. Many of the features on Christmas cards originated in different countries such as the poinsettia (Mexico and the Caribbean), the log (France), Santa Claus (America), the decorated tree (Germany).
✧ Find Christmas greetings in other languages and make a display start with: Oiche Nodlaig Mhaith (Irish); Joyeux Noel (French); Feliz Navidad (Spanish); Kala Christougenna (Greek); Nadolig Llawen (Welsh); Buon Natale (Italian).

LISTEN CAREFULLY

Objective

English – To listen to and tell stories.

Group size

Whole group, small group and individual.

What you need

Cassette recorder (which can record onto blank cassettes), selection of short pantomime and Christmas stories in books.

Preparation

Read and record a popular pantomime story from a book onto a blank tape. Have the book containing clear pictures ready to show the children.

What to do

Play your recording of a popular pantomime story such as Jack and the Beanstalk or Babes in the Wood to the whole group while showing them the illustrations to accompany the text.

Divide the children into smaller working groups and working with one group at a time, take them into a quiet area and read a short Christmas story to them. Ask them to work as a group to retell and record the story on to cassette, while you show them the illustrations. Let the children take it in turns so that they all have a chance to talk. Be flexible in the time you spend with each group and the degree of prompting required, depending on the needs of each child. Stress that they must all listen carefully to the other children in the group.

Play back the cassette so the children can enjoy listening to their version of the story.

Discussion

Talk about the stories that are normally associated with pantomimes. Have any of the children been to see a pantomime? Explain briefly how a recording is made, showing them the microphone, switches and tape. Some children will be familiar with cassette tapes and making recordings already. Talk about taking turns and respecting other children by listening to their contributions. Ask children for their suggestions for follow-up activities. Which stories would they like to tell?

Follow-up activities

✧ Encourage the children to make some illustrations for the story and write captions to go with them.
✧ Transcribe the children's stories and type them up to present to the whole group.
✧ Encourage children to make up and record their own stories.
✧ Start telling a story to a group of children and ask them to predict what will happen next.
✧ Listen to a story in an unfamiliar language using a wide variety of props and aids. Can the children still follow the story?

HOW DO DECORATIONS WORK?

Objective

Science – To encourage enquiry through examining Christmas decorations.

Group size

Pairs.

What you need

Half of an old hollow ball, Plasticine, selection of card and sugar paper, short garden cane, string, very small hoop or circle of wire, pencil, two-coloured thick foil, scissors, colouring materials, sticky tape, adhesive, glitter (optional).

Preparation

Cut pieces of string ready for the mobile – one piece to suspend it, two long and two short pieces to hang the decorations. Cut the foil into strips of approximately 1cm wide and 30cm long. Create simple card templates of a Christmas tree and bauble (each tree will require two outlines and each mobile will require four identical bauble shapes). Help the children to draw round the tree and bauble templates on thin card or sugar paper and cut them out.

What to do

Mobile – To make a mobile, decorate four identical baubles (using the card templates) on both sides. The children can use any form of decoration as long as it does not alter the weight significantly. Hang up the cane from the central point and attach strings to the baubles. Attach one long and one short string to each end of the cane. Move the strings until the cane balances.

Christmas tree – Invite the children to decorate their tree shapes (cut out from the card templates) in any way they like, using their choice of craft materials from those available. When the decoration is completed, attach the small stick to the base of one of the tree shapes and stick the second tree shape to the first. Place a ball of Plasticine in the base of a half ball and stand the completed tree in the Plasticine.

Foil decoration – Wrap a strip of foil around the length of the pencil (make sure you get the angle right at the beginning). Remove the pencil and loosen the foil slightly. Make several twists in the same way and hang them from the small hoop.

Discussion

Talk about the suitability of all the materials used to make the decorations. Why do we need to be careful about where we put the decorations when we make the mobile? What happens if the strings are moved? Is the length of the strings important? Why do the children think the Christmas tree wobbles? How much force do they need to exert to make it fall over? How can they change that? Why does the foil appear to spin? What happens if it is placed over a heat source such as a radiator? What causes that? What do they think will happen if they change the materials used or the sizes of the decorations?

Follow-up activities

✧ Use the decorations at Christmas time.
✧ Experiment with the children's suggestions for different materials, shapes and sizes.
✧ Try making other decorations with a scientific bias such as a snowstorm or fridge magnets.

ADVENT CALENDAR

Objective

Mathematics – To count the days to Christmas.

Group size

Whole group.

What you need

Selection of card, baubles, candles, adhesive, scissors, sticky tape, hoop, red and green crêpe paper, string, small sticky labels, 24 small boxes (such as small Smarties or raisin boxes), gift wrap, decorative materials such as braid or coloured foil.

Preparation

Number the labels 1 – 24. Cut out 24 different bauble shapes, place these in the boxes and gift-wrap each one. Tie string around the boxes leaving approximately 20 – 25cm to tie to the hoop.

What to do

Decorate the hoop with strips of red and green crêpe paper. Tie the parcels so they are evenly spaced around the hoop. Use the labels to number the boxes in random order. Suspend the hoop in a suitable space.

Starting on December 1 let one child open a box each day. Once the child has opened the 'parcel' and taken out the bauble shape, encourage them to use a variety of materials to decorate their bauble. When complete the decorated baubles can all be hung on the Christmas tree.

Use the 'opening' as an opportunity for counting activities such as counting with odd and even numbers, adding on one, counting backwards and number recognition.

Discussion

Talk about the preparations for Christmas. Explain that many of our Christmas customs came from Germany, including Advent calendars. Talk about periods of time. Start with the day of the week that relates directly to this activity. What other periods of time do they know? Have they ever heard an adult say: 'Wait a minute'? How long is a minute? How do we mark a day or a week? How do they know that a new week has started? Talk about the names of the days of the week.

Follow-up activities

✧ Write Merry Christmas in German for display near the wreath – Froehliche Weihnachten

✧ Make individual Advent candle calendars by marking a picture of a large candle into 24 divisions. Colour one division for each day.

✧ Give everyday maths activities a Christmas flavour: use pictures associated with Christmas for counting and sorting; join numbers to form a Christmas shape; look at the symmetry in a snowflake; draw half a bell and ask the children to complete it.

✧ Make an Advent wreath, adding a candle on each of the four weeks before Christmas.

THE CHRISTMAS STORY

Objective

Religious Education – To introduce Christmas as a religious festival.

Group size

Whole group.

What you need

Models of a stable, manger, animals and characters in the story, a Bible.

Preparation

Prepare the characters if you are not using commercially produced ones, and put them in the correct order.

What to do

Explain that you are going to tell the children a story that is special for Christians which comes from the Holy Bible. Show them the Bible and explain that it should be handled carefully.

Explain that you are going to tell them the story of the birth of a very special baby called Jesus. Tell the story of the Nativity using the stable, manger and characters at the appropriate times. Tell the children that it is because of Jesus' birth that we celebrate Christmas to remember his birthday.

Discussion

Explain that December 25 is not the actual date of Jesus' birth as nobody is really sure when it was. In some countries Christmas is celebrated in January. How do the children celebrate their birthdays? Many Christians like to start the celebrations by going to Church. Have any of the children been to Church? Discuss their experiences. Think about people who find it difficult to celebrate Christmas such as the old and lonely, people who have to work or help others on that day. How can they celebrate? What can we do to let them know that they are remembered? Talk about the Wise Men taking gifts to Jesus.

Follow-up activities

✧ Learn songs that tell the story of Christmas.
✧ Use photocopiable page 93 for the children to sequence the pictures and retell the Christmas story.
✧ Act the story using simple props and costumes.
✧ Invite a representative of the local Church to talk to the children about Christmas.
✧ Read A New Baby for Christmas on page 69.

FAMILY TRADITIONS

Objectives

History – To learn about Christmas in the past.

Group size

Whole group.

What you need

Paper, art materials, scissors, adhesive, writing materials, potatoes, knife and paint.

Preparation

Write a letter to the children's families asking for any memories of how parents and grandparents celebrated Christmas. Ask them to think about decorations, food, games, visitors and songs. Prepare a potato print to represent each category.

What to do

Share the replies which you receive with the whole group. Ask the children to record the responses in a variety of ways – copy writing, drawing, painting, reproducing decorations, cutting and sticking.

Cut out the responses and sort them into the separate categories such as decorations, food and so on and make them into separate books. To add interest make each book in a relevant shape such as a tree or a present. Help the children to arrange their work in the books and show them how to use the potato prints to make decorative borders for their covers. Although it might not be possible to include all the children's work ensure that every child makes a contribution. Show the completed books to their families and thank them for their contributions.

Discussion

Talk about the replies you get and discuss how the customs are similar or different to present day celebrations? Were any of the memories from outside your area or from wartime? Discuss which customs the children are familiar with. Talk about giving and receiving presents. Who would they like to give a present to and what would it be? Discuss the friends and families who we visit during the celebrations and about sharing happy occasions.

Follow-up activities

✧ Learn some Christmas songs and perform them for families or a group of elderly people. Make some percussion instruments to accompany the singing and decorate them with red and green.
✧ Visit local shops and talk about the ways in which they decorate and prepare for Christmas.
✧ Make cards and gift-wrap using traditional Christmas designs.
✧ Find out about some of the stories attached to the pictures on Christmas cards such as the robin who fanned the flames to keep Baby Jesus warm and scorched his breast; the weeds that turned into poinsettias as the poor child gave her gift to the crib in Mexico.
✧ Read the poem It's Christmas Time on page 68.

CHAPTER 5 CHINESE NEW YEAR

Lively and colourful celebrations involving dance, music, cooking and craft are all part of the Chinese New Year. Make decorations, cook a stir-fry and act out the story with the activities in this chapter

LION DANCE

Objective

PE – To think about the ways that different animals (both real and fictional) move and to imitate them.

Group size

Whole group.

What you need

Large space to enable all the children to move freely and safely, one hoop between every two children, tambourine to give signals (optional), cassette tape and video of 'Lion Dance' music (BBC Watch video) (optional), copy of the story of the Chinese New Year (page 85).

Preparation

Tell the story from page 85 of the animals' race across the river. If possible, watch a video of lion dancing together – point out to the children how the head is held. Place the hoops in strategic places around the room so that the children can obtain them quickly and easily.

What to do

Start with a warm-up to include activities in which the children must obey commands such as stop, go, change direction and make movements which are high/low, fast/slow, and large/small.

Remind the children of the story and ask them to think how the animals would move? Experiment with different movements for the rat, ox, rabbit, snake, monkey, cockerel and dragons. Ask them to each choose one animal and to work concentrating on the actions for that animal.

Ask the children to recall the video of lion dancing and tell them to try to reproduce the movements while you play some appropriate music. Tell the children to find partners, to share a hoop with their partner and to experiment with lion dancing using the hoop as the lion's head. Let half the group watch while the others perform their dance and then repeat with the other group.

Discussion

Explain that lion dancing is just one of the ways that the Chinese New Year is celebrated with processions where the dancing is accompanied by drums, gongs and symbols. Traditionally, the lions accompany a huge dragon as it dances along the road. Some shops and houses hang money (wrapped in red) from upstairs windows. The dancers then 'climb' up to collect it. It is hoped that the music will chase away evil spirits and that the dancing will encourage good luck during the following year. Talk about working together, taking turns, and listening to each other's ideas.

Follow-up activities

- Encourage the children to accompany their movements with musical instruments.
- Join the pairs together to form longer 'lions'.
- Decorate the hoop to resemble the head and use a decorated hoop for the body.
- Use the 'dances' as part of a performance, assembly or other form of celebration.

CUT PAPER WORK

Objective

Art – To make decorations using folding and cutting skills.

Group size

Up to six children.

What you need

Scissors, adhesive, red and yellow strips of paper approximately 10 x 30cm – one for each child and one extra set, a copy of the story of the Chinese New Year (page 85).

Preparation

Cut the paper to size. Tell the story of the Chinese New Year and explain some of the ways in which it is celebrated.

What to do

Ask each child to choose a piece of paper and show them how to make a concertina fold. Repeat slowly allowing the children to make their own. The number of folds will depend on the development of individual children.

Then show how you can cut the folded paper and emphasise the importance of only cutting part of the way across. Let the children make their own cuts on both sides of their folded paper. Open the sheet to reveal a cut pattern. Carefully put adhesive around the edge of the paper and mount it onto a contrasting colour to display.

Discussion

Talk about times when the children decorate their homes. How do their families prepare for a celebration? What do they celebrate? How can children help when preparations are taking place? Encourage children to discuss the parts they like and dislike. Discuss the need to fold the paper neatly and cut carefully, what do they think will happen if they don't? Why must they be careful with scissors? Can they think of any rules for using them? Cut paper work is a traditional Chinese art: discuss the need for great accuracy and attention to detail when making really intricate animal designs. Do red and yellow go well together?

Follow-up activities

- Use the shapes to make a New Year card.
- Make similar patterns out of tissue-paper and place on a window so that the light can show through.
- Set up a red and gold interest table.
- Examine other forms of Chinese art and writing.

RUNNING THE RACE

Objective

English – To listen to a story and act it out using simple props.

Group size

At least 14.

What you need

Card, scissors, crayons, rolled newspaper holders for the masks (or elastic if the children are happy to wear them), copy of the Chinese New Year Story (page 85), strips of blue and green fabric or crêpe paper (if there are more than 14 children).

Preparation

Clear a space to act out the story. Read the story. Make masks for each of the animals and Gods in the story. The children can draw and make their own masks or you may have some animal mask templates to use. Let the children decorate their own masks – the extent of the decoration will depend on the time and materials available, and the skills of the children.

If there are more than 14 children cut long strips of fabric for some children to hold to form the river. Place all the masks – upside down – in the order that the animals completed the race.

What to do

Read the story again and give the children plenty of opportunity to discuss and ask questions. Explain that you are going to retell the story with the children acting the various parts. Talk about the characters and the kind of movements they are likely to make.

Ask the children to stand in a space where they can see you easily. Tell the story with pauses at appropriate times for the actions to take place. On the first run-through 'swimming' can take place on the spot using appropriate arm movements.

Now allocate 'parts'. These need not necessarily be speaking parts – it depends on the confidence of the children.

As you reach the race in the story ask the children forming the river to move their strips slowly up and down. The 'swimmers' step over these one-by-one. Younger children might find it difficult to finish the race in the 'correct' order. This is not essential, but try and make sure that the rat and the ox finish first and second respectively!

Discussion

How do the children think that the ox felt when it was tricked by the rat?

Does it matter who wins the race? Explain that all the animals have years named after them – even the one that came last. Talk about ways in which the New Year is celebrated now. There are street processions with lion dancing. It is a time for new beginnings with new clothes, settling of debts, special foods (dumplings) and lucky bags containing money are given to children for good fortune. These celebrations take place in Chinese communities all over the world.

Follow-up activities

✧ Develop the roles of the children – perhaps looking at the type of movements or giving them speaking roles.
✧ Use the story as the basis for an Assembly or to perform to the children's families.
✧ Prepare a class book of the story using the children's own words and either their pictures or photographs of them in their roles (gain parental consent to do this).
✧ Read the poem Carnival Time on page 70.
✧ Sing the song Chinese New Year on page 78, to accompany the story.

ANIMAL ANTICS

Objective

Science – To observe and describe the characteristics of different animals.

Group size

Whole group followed by small groups.

What you need

Variety of pictures of animals, books containing clear pictures of animals and if possible an adult who can bring in a pet.

Preparation

Contact local people who are particularly interested in animals and invite them in to meet the children and answer their questions. Arrange for an adult to bring a pet to show the group (make sure the pet can be safely viewed by the children).

What to do

Remind the children of the animals in the Chinese New Year story. What do the children know about them? Have a close look at the pet in the classroom. How does it move? Where does it live? What does it eat? How big does it grow?

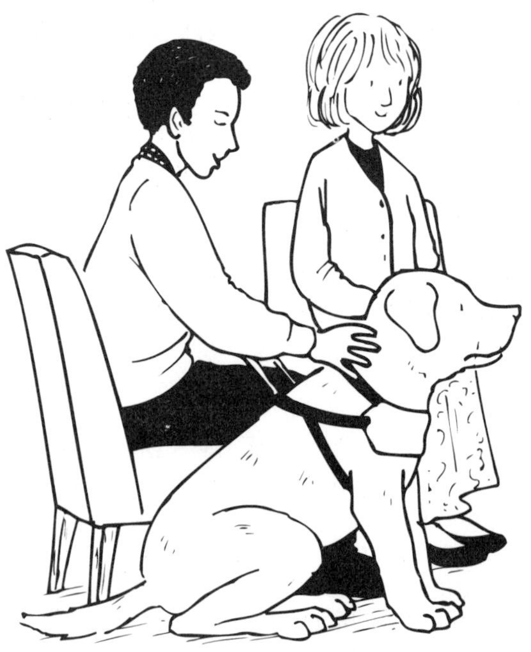

Choose a few animals from the story, such as the rat, tiger, cockerel and snake, and try to answer these same questions for these animals. Repeat the activity with the dragon. How do the answers compare? Do all the children agree with the 'information' about the dragon? Use the reference books and photographs to check information.

Work with one small group at a time to answer similar questions for the other animals. Encourage the children to question and find out as much as they can from any sources. Make constructive use of local expertise for this activity by asking knowledgeable adults for information which is just as valid as looking in a book!

Discussion

Throughout the activity encourage the children to question. If you don't know the answer to a certain question, find the answers together using the reference books available. Discuss the suitability of animals as pets. Why is it rare to have a tiger as a pet? Which animals are real and which are imaginary? How can we tell the difference? Can the children think of any stories containing imaginary animals? Talk about the children's own experiences with animals. What can they tell you?

Follow-up activities

✧ Paint pictures of the animals and their habitats.
✧ Read stories about dragons and ask the children to draw what they think a dragon looks like.
✧ Make a pictogram of the children's favourite animals from the story.
✧ Collect the animal pictures and information together in a group book.

CHINESE MUSIC

Objective

Music – To listen to and enjoy Chinese music.

Group size

Whole or half group.

What you need

Some Chinese music on cassette, CD or record and facilities for playing the music, a copy of the Chinese New Year story (page 85).

Preparation

Acquire some suitable music – it might be available from the local community, a multi-cultural resource centre or the local library. Listen to the music and select suitable pieces. Set up the equipment so that it is only necessary to switch on.

What to do

Remind the children of the Chinese New Year story, reading it through again if necessary, and discuss together all the ways of celebrating. Talk about the music used for the lion dancing and how it is different from most of the music the children are likely to hear on the radio, for example.

Ask the children to sit in a comfortable position. Some might find it easier to concentrate if they close their eyes. Listen to a short piece of Chinese music together and watch the children's reactions. Afterwards, discuss it and ask the children to think about what movements they would make to the music. Would it be fast, slow, small steps or large steps? Listen to a contrasting piece of music, choose a quiet piece this time and discuss . Finally, ask the children to close their eyes and listen to some more music– just for pleasure.

Discussion

Talk about how a piece of music makes the children feel. Some parts might be slow and dreamy while others are loud and aggressive. Which words can they use to describe the piece? What do they think about when they hear it? Explain that music plays a central role in the processions and celebrations with a large drum playing a leading part. Can the children distinguish the drum in the pieces played? What other types of instruments can they hear?

Follow-up activities

✧ Let the children dance to the music if they wish – or use hand movements as an accompaniment.
✧ Try a percussion accompaniment, perhaps using drums or tambourines, either made by the children or commercially produced.
✧ Sing a Chinese New Year song (see page 78), and learn to say 'Kung hey fat choy' (Happy New Year!).
✧ Play the Chinese music as background music while the children are busy with other Chinese New Year activities.

MIX AND MATCH

Objective

Mathematics – To encourage observation and discussion of different attributes and to match pictures of animals according to these attributes.

Group size

Up to six children.

What you need

Photocopiable page 94, showing pictures of the animals in the story, a set of 2D shapes.

Preparation

Copy the animal pictures you have on to individual cards and colour them. Discuss the attributes of different shapes and sort and match shapes such as squares, triangles and circles according to shape, size and colour as an introduction to sorting by attributes.

What to do

Show the animal cards to the children and talk about the features of the different animals. Ask them to find matching pairs according to specific attributes such as length of tail, size of ears or colour of coat. Start by matching the obvious attributes and then encourage them to observe more obscure similarities.

Ask the children to work in pairs to find pairs of animals taking it in turns to set the tasks. One child may ask the other: 'Please find two animals with short legs' and then the other may ask: 'Please find two animals with horns'.

Discussion

Talk about how the animals' distinctive features suit their particular lifestyles. Which animals enjoy swimming? What features make it easy to swim? At the beginning of the story the animals were discussing their differences and arguing. The New Year is a time for people to settle disputes and be kind and thoughtful to others. Discuss ways of being kind to each other and why we should be willing to say, 'I'm sorry'.

Follow-up activities

✧ Find out more about the animals in the story and how they live.
✧ Match animals that have similar features of lifestyle such as 'all pets' or 'all eat grass'.
✧ Play 'What am I?'. There are two ways to play this game, one is for a child to describe an animal and their partner must work out which animal it is, the second game is for one child to ask questions of their partner to determine the animal: 'Does it have four legs?' – 'Yes'; 'Does it have a long tail?' – 'Yes'; 'Is it smaller than me?' – 'No'; 'Is it a horse?' – 'Yes!'.
✧ Paint some colouful pictures of the animals and display them in the correct order.

GOOD LUCK DECORATIONS

Objective

Design and Technology – To make classroom decorations using a range of design-and-make skills.

Group size

Whole group divided into four.

What you need

Adhesive, scissors, sticky tape, twigs, yoghurt pots, Plasticine, stiff paper, contrasting fabric and pre-cut frames, pink tissue-paper, red, gold and yellow paper, paint – especially red, gold, yellow, brown, gold braid, small pieces of different papers and fabrics – especially red, gold and yellow, decorative materials in the appropriate colours such as sequins, glitter, gift wrap.

Preparation

Prepare greeting card frames and prepare sheets for Lucky Bags. Make an example of the blossom tree, card, banner and lucky bags following the instructions below. Show children the completed examples and discuss how they are made. Explain that the children are going to make their own decorations using these basic designs but decorating them as they like. Divide the children into four groups and explain that each group will make a different decoration.

What to do

Lucky bags – cut out the lucky bag outline. Show the children how to fold, slowly and carefully, along the dotted lines. Put adhesive on the shaded areas and stick down to form a lucky bag. Encourage them to make a decoration, such as blossom, cut paper design, gold pattern or the animal for the year and to stick this decoration to the centre of the bag.
Blossom trees – decorate the yoghurt pots in a variety of ways. Push a piece of Plasticine into the base of each pot – large enough to support some twigs. Tear pink tissue paper into pieces approximately 6cm square and crumple the centre of the paper to form flower shapes. Stick the blossom to the twigs and stand the 'blossom trees' in the decorated pots.
Greeting cards – carefully fold the card in half. Paint stems and pink blossom on the contrasting fabric. When dry, stick the painting to the outside of the card. Cover with the pre-cut frame and stick in place. On the inside, write 'Happy New Year', or 'Kung hey fat choy'.
Banner – copy the Chinese greeting (above) on to yellow paper and cut out. Stick it on to the centre of a red piece of paper. Decorate the border in a variety of ways such as with gold braid, small flowers cut from gift wrap, small pink blossom, red and gold glitter, pieces of foil.

Discussion

Discuss the way in which whole cities or districts of cities are decorated for the Chinese celebrations. In some areas there are street processions with decorated floats and lion dancing. Homes are thoroughly cleaned before being decorated with symbols of good luck such as banners, peach blossom, lions and dragons. People exchange cards and give children 'lucky money' from both lucky bags and branches hung with money. Do the preparations remind the children of any other festival preparations?

Follow-up activities

✧ Make lanterns from red and gold gift wrap around a cardboard tube covered with yellow paper.
✧ Make a mobile using the symbols of the festival or the animals in the story. Hang from a hoop decorated in red and gold. Attach red and gold tissue paper streamers.
✧ Make a dragon wall picture – make the body from large circles of paper or foil decorated with scraps of material. Cut spikes of paper for the back, add feet, a tail and head. Make the eyes using half a ball of the appropriate size.

CHINESE STIR FRY

Objective

Technology – To prepare, cook and share Chinese food.

Group size

Whole group divided into groups of 2–3 with an adult working with each small group.

What you need

Rice: two cups rice, two tbsp oil, one tbsp salt, two and a half cups of water – the amount of water will vary according to the type of rice used.
Stir-fry: ingredients will vary according to the vegetables you have available and the quantity of stir fry required. One carrot, three spring onions, 50g mushrooms, one courgette, 50g beansprouts, one green pepper, two tbsp soy sauce. Saucepan, wok or large frying pan, suitable surfaces, knives to chop vegetables, aprons, source of heat, washing-up facilities, colanders, covered bag or bin to dispose of waste, dishes, forks, serving spoons and chopsticks.

Preparation

Ask some parents to assist by helping you to cook with the children. Purchase ingredients and collect together all the resources required. Talk to volunteers about health and safety issues. Check the safety of the cooker and its position, ensure that all cooking surfaces are clean. Make sure that all the adults involved understand the arrangements for the session and the discussion points.

Explain to the children that they are going to cook a co-operative Chinese meal as part of their Chinese New Year celebration. Ask them to prepare for it by washing hands thoroughly, wearing aprons and tying hair back.

What to do

Ask an adult working with a small group to take responsibility for cooking the rice – involving the children at different stages so that they can see the changes that take place as it is cooked. Wash and drain the rice, then put the rice, salt and oil in a large saucepan. Add the water and cover. Bring the water to the boil then lower the heat and cook for approximately 12 more minutes. Distribute the vegetables and knives so that each small group can take part in the preparation. (The adults might need to cut the carrots and remove the seeds from the pepper.) When all the vegetables are ready, ask everyone to sit down out of the way while one person heats the oil in the wok. When the oil is hot add the carrots and cook for two minutes, and then add the other ingredients carefully. Keep stirring while they cook for approximately five minutes. While the food is cooking involve the children in clearing up the room and preparing to eat. Share the food so that everyone has a taste. Ask children to help in tidying up and thank all the adults for their assistance.

Discussion

Talk about health and safety issues. Why do the children think that it is important to have clean hands and surfaces? Why must they be very careful about the cooker and hot oil? Why do they think the food is cut into thin strips? Why were the carrots cooked first? What happens to the rice as it is cooked? Discuss the children's observations. Talk about the name 'stir-fry'. Why do the children think that this dish has that name. At Chinese New Year families might eat a special rice pudding full of fruits and nuts to symbolise good luck. Dumplings are also prepared as a symbol of wealth. Can the children think of any foods they eat that are symbolic?

Follow-up activities

✧ Cook or purchase other foods that are eaten during the festival such as Nin Ko, Chin duy or Yaukot, and enjoy these together.
✧ Grow bean sprouts.
✧ Try instant noodles or prawn crackers – watch for any changes as they cook.
✧ Identify soy sauce, spring onions and ginger by using the sense of smell.

CHAPTER 6
SPECIAL DAYS

Throughout the year there are a number of one-day festivals which children regularly take part in. This chapter provides one activity for each of these festivals to complete the autumn and winter programme of events.

ETHIOPIAN NEW YEAR

Objective

Art – To make a star of David using the Rastafarian colours.

Group size

Whole group.

What you need

Black backing paper, adhesive, red, green and gold glitter, for each star – six split pins and two strips of red, green and gold card approximately 10 × 1.5 cm.

Preparation

Cut the strips and round the ends.

What to do

To make a star of David take three strips, one in each of the three colours. Fix them together with split pins to form a triangle. To make the second triangle join two different colours together and weave these through the first triangle so that they only cross different colours. Weave the third piece through and join with split pins. Position the triangles to form a star of David and stick in position.

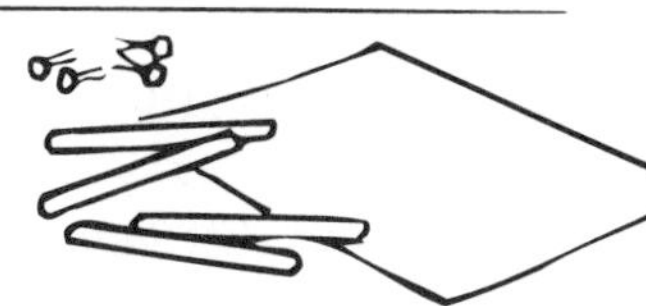

Dot with adhesive and sprinkle with glitter of the appropriate colour. Make a border around the display paper by sprinkling red, green and gold glitter around the edge. Display the completed stars on the black background.

Discussion

Explain that many of the Rastafarian traditions are associated with Ethiopia and Jamaica. The colours in the star are all in the Ethiopian flag and symbolise blood (struggle), the sun and the earth. The other symbol of Rastafarianism is the Lion of Judah. Festivals are generally celebrated by friends and families gathering together for exhibitions, drumming, dancing and food. Talk about the music that might be played during the festival which starts on September 11. The music of Bob Marley and reggae grew out of the tradition of Rastafarian drumming and chanting. Discuss the food that might be eaten: strict Rastafarians only eat natural and organic food – often vegetarian but definitely not pork.

Follow-up activities

✧ Make some food that is suitable for Rastafarians to eat such as banana bread or fruit punch. Caribbean food such as yam, plantain or cho-cho would also be suitable.
✧ Design and make a flag or badge using the Rastafarian colours.
✧ Thread red, yellow and green beads in a repetitive pattern, and make necklaces.
✧ Make home-made drums and decorate with black, red, gold and green.
✧ Use African print fabric to make dolls' and dressing-up clothes.
✧ The festival takes place very near the new school year; discuss ways to mark a new year and a new start.

SUKKOT / FEAST OF TABERNACLES

Objective

Geography – To plan a processional route around the room.

Group size

Up to six children.

What you need

Drawings of the main features of a room such as the window, door, tables, role-play area, books, sand tray. Large sheet of plain paper, Blu-Tack.

Preparation

Prepare the pencil sketches of the main features of the room.

What to do

Tell the children that you are going to take a walk around the room and that you would like them to follow you in a procession.

The route could be something like: around the sand tray, between the window and the table, through the 'hospital', in front of the book shelf and past the door.

Now ask them to think of another route that they could take. Let them use the pictures to help describe their route. When they have made a final decision, record it and illustrate it with the pencil sketches.

Repeat the activity with other groups of children and compare ideas. Children can follow the routes planned by another group.

Discussion

Explain that at the end of the festival the Torah is carried in procession around the Synagogue. The festival itself, which takes place in late September – early October, is a reminder of the 40 years in which the Jewish people travelled in the wilderness and lived in temporary shelters. To remember this time, Jewish people build temporary shelters either at home or at the Synagogue. Talk about the importance of having a route or plan. Have any of the children seen adults using a plan or a map? Talk about the use of the terms such as 'between', 'behind' and so on.

Follow-up activities

✧ Make a temporary shelter from a strong cardboard box. Make the roof from branches and leaves. Decorate it with pictures of fruit and add dolls' house furniture.
✧ Make a temporary shelter in the home corner.
✧ Tell stories that involve a route such as *Rosie's Walk*, Pat Hutchins (Picture Puffin).

GRANDPARENTS' DAY

Objective
History – To find out about daily life in the children's grandparents' childhood.

Group size
Up to 15 children in each group.

What you need
Comfortable chair, adult scribe with a notebook or a cassete recorder

Preparation
Invite the children's grandparents to take part in the activity. Discuss any topics which would be appropriate to talk about and ask if they have any artefacts that the children could handle. Ask if they are they willing to have a photograph taken. Explain that you would like to record some of the discussion for a display later. Arrange convenient times for the visitors.

Tell the children that they are going to have a special guest and involve them in preparing the area to be used. Explain that it is to celebrate Grandparents' Day which is a fairly new festival taking place in September. Talk to them about your own childhood, pointing out any things which show how it is different to theirs.

What to do
On the day of the visit ask a small group of children to welcome the grandparent(s). Seat your visitor comfortably and settle the children quietly.

Invite the visitor to talk to the children about their memories, or any topics you may have discussed together which are of particular interest. Tell the children to sit quietly and to listen carefully, but give them the opportunity to ask questions. You may need to guide them or prompt relevant (and polite) questions. If the grandparent has bought in any artefacts which the children can look at, let the children handle them and see if they can determine how they were used if appropriate or display them where the children can see clearly.

Afterwards write a letter of thanks to any grandparents who have given you their time.

Discussion
What is a grandparent? How do they fit into our family structure? Remember that some children's grandparents might have died, live far away or be estranged from the children so consider the individual circumstances of your children and don't make assumptions about their family circumstances. Consider together: what is old? Are all grandparents old? Can grandparents be active and still at work? What names do they call their grandparents? What is the most popular name used? Where did their grandparents live as children? If they moved house – why? What was everyday life like, consider: food, clothes, TV, entertainment, games, cars? Can anyone remember life without cars, TV and hamburgers?

Follow-up activities
✧ Hold a party for all grandparents. Invite them to play with the children and provide a drink, a snack and entertain them with a song. Arrange to 'borrow' a grandparent for any children who are unable to provide their own.
✧ Display photographs and written comments to record the activity.
✧ Visit a toy museum.
✧ Paint pictures of grandparents and / or artefacts.
✧ Prepare an exhibition of everyday objects, photographs and so on in grandparents' childhood. Help the children to prepare their own labels.

GURU NANAK'S BIRTHDAY

Objective

Religious Education – To encourage children to value caring and sharing.

Group size

Up to six.

What you need

Space to sit in a circle.

What to do

Join the children to sit together in a circle and explain that you would like them to talk to the person next to them about someone who has been kind to them. They need to listen carefully to each other because they are then going to be asked to share what they have heard with the rest of the group.

Think together about ways that we can all be kind to each other. Ask each child to think of something that they can do to be helpful either at home or in the group.

Start with the child next to you, ask them to say what she/he can do. The next child repeats this and adds what she/he can do. Continue around the circle until it comes back to you and you have to repeat what each child can do.

Discussion

Explain that Guru Nanak believed that everyone is equally important. It doesn't make any difference how rich you are – you should still be kind and thoughtful. The free kitchens in Sikh Gurdwaras are based on his teaching – everyone helps and everyone shares. He was a very kind man who is reputed to always have had time to listen. He lived at a time when there was considerable conflict in India and it was his greatest wish to have peace.

Guru Nanak is very special to Sikh people and you will often find pictures of him in their homes and Gurdwaras. Who is special to the children? Do they have photographs of special people? During the celebrations, the Holy Book (The Guru Granth Sahib) is read continuously from start to finish and the Golden Temple at Amritsar is illuminated. The celebrations take place in November.

Follow-up activities

- ✧ Tell stories of people who have been kind and helpful such as Florence Nightingale, Mary Seacole and Mother Teresa.
- ✧ Make a wish for someone.
- ✧ Think of ways to make new children feel welcome in your group.
- ✧ Play co-operative games.

BONFIRE NIGHT

Objective

Art – To produce a group picture using a variety of techniques.

Group size

Whole group divided into groups of three or four.

What you need

Large sheet of black background paper, black paper for fireworks, glitter in a variety of colours – especially silver and gold, cardboard tubes, foil stars, sticky tape, adhesive, orange or yellow nylon rope, tissue paper in a variety of colours, powder paint, salt, flour, squeezy bottle, pictures of fireworks (optional).

Preparation

Cut the cardboard tube to a suitable length for the size of the picture and then in half vertically. Cut curves of black paper, cut a spiral of black paper, mix some thick paint with glitter. Mix half a cup of dry paint with a teaspoon of salt, mix equal amounts of flour and salt – mix with powder paint and water – put it in the squeezy bottle. Mount the background paper on to a wall.

What to do

Put the children into small groups and allocate each group a different task. One group can cover the cardboard tube with paper and stick it on to the background to make a firework shape. Then stick foil stars with a small piece of sticky tape to the background to look as though they are showering out of the tube firework.

Using the illustrations here as a guide, ask groups of children to create different firework effects, by using a combination of paint, glitter, salt and glue mixtures. For example, the mixture in the squeezy bottle can be used to create a 'shower' effect onto curves of black paper, the black paper spiral can be sprinkled with glitter on to glue and so on.

Ask another group of children to cover pieces of the cardboard tube with paper and stick them to the background. Cut out some flame-shaped pieces of tissue paper and crinkle them up to stick inside the tubes and fix to the background. Ask the children to use a combination of colours to look like flames or make a series of fireworks to resemble 'traffic lights'.

When all of the individual fireworks are dry, mount them on to the black background. Involve the children in assembling the picture.

Discussion

Talk about when (November 5) and why Bonfire Night is celebrated and some of the customs associated with it (see page 6). Have all the children seen a bonfire and fireworks? Can they describe the fireworks? How do they look, sound and make you feel? Emphasise the safety aspects of bonfire night and of taking part in properly organised events. Reinforce the fact that children should never handle fireworks or go too near bonfires. Stress this strongly but without frightening the children too much.

Follow-up activities

✧ Produce the group's own Firework Code. If possible, photocopy these and send them home.
✧ Make a group bonfire picture using sticks and tissue paper.
✧ Make pin-wheel sandwiches to look like Catherine wheels and share them together.

NEW YEAR'S DAY

Objective

English – To write some new year resolutions.

Group size

Whole group with individual work.

What you need

Photograph of each child (with parental consent), group book with a page for each child.

Preparation

Take a photograph of each child or collect them from home and make up a group book with each page containing a child's photograph, their name and a resolution. To add interest, the book could be made in the shape of the year (for example, 1998).

What to do

Introduce the activity by asking any adults in the group to explain some of their resolutions. Ask the children to consider what resolutions they would like to make. Let them record their suggestions on their special page in your class book.

Some children might find it helpful for you to write 'I will try to...' for them to complete. Other children may be able to write their sentences by themselves. The amount of assistance needed will obviously vary depending on the writing skills of the individual children in your group.

When the book is complete share it with the whole group. Put it in the book corner for the children to look through when they have a chance.

Discussion

Traditions on New Year's Eve include first-footing (a dark male stranger enters the house carrying coal for good luck), eating black bun, visiting Trafalgar Square or listening to bagpipes. Many people sing 'Auld Lang Syne'. Perhaps you could invite someone in to tell you about any local customs. Discuss any activities that the children can remember from the previous year. What was particularly enjoyable? Was there anything that made them feel proud? Talk about the new year being seen as a chance to start again.

Follow-up activities

✧ Make a list of group resolutions. Record them on a large sheet and display them as a reminder.
✧ New Year is particularly celebrated in Scotland and is often associated with bagpipes. Listen to a march on the bagpipes and process around the room to the beat.
✧ The New Year is often 'rung in' with church bells. Encourage the children to listen to the bells in the local church. Why do they think they are being played? Find out how they make the sound.

ST VALENTINE'S DAY

Objective

Art – To make heart-shaped patterns using a variety of textures and techniques.

Group size

Up to six children.

What you need

Adhesive, scissors, paper and card of different textures, sheets of clear plastic, potatoes and thick red paint for printing, red, pink and white tissue paper, paper for printing on to, decorative materials such as wool, glitter or braid.

Preparation

Halve the potatoes and cut heart shapes in them. Cut out plenty of small heart shapes from red paper – all of the same size. Also cut heart shapes in a wide range of sizes, shades and textures. Put spare materials so that the children can select and prepare their own heart shapes.

What to do

Provide a selection of heart-shapes in a variety of sizes, shades and textures for the children to work with. Ask them to arrange them on a sheet of clear plastic. Older children can try arranging the shapes in patterns and cutting out further shapes of their own. They can also add wool, ribbon or glitter to complete their pattern.

Use the potatoes to print heart shapes making patterns. If the children work carefully they can fit the printing together to form tessellations.

Give each child a selection of the small heart shapes, some paper and adhesive and encourage them to experiment with making different patterns. When they are happy with one design they can stick it into place on the paper.

Discussion

Talk about the heart shape and the symmetry involved. Explain that whatever happens to one side should also happen to the other. Discuss the texture of materials. Encourage the children to feel and describe them. How do they look when the light shines through them? Will it shine through all of the materials? What kinds of patterns can be made? What are the easiest ways to fit them together?

Discuss when St Valentine's Day is (February 14) and what happens (people often give cards to people who are special to them – without signing them so that it is a mystery). This custom is thought to have originated from a story about St. Valentine who refused to obey the Emperor Claudius who banned marriage for soldiers. Valentine felt that this was too harsh and he was imprisoned and eventually killed. While in prison he became friendly with the jailer's daughter.

After his death it was said that a note was found saying, 'From your Valentine'. He was killed in the night before the festival of Lupercalia when traditionally young people drew lots to determine their future partner.

Follow-up activities

✧ Make biscuits, sandwiches, peppermint creams or cakes in heart shapes.
✧ Make Valentine hats by decorating large cardboard hearts with red, white and pink materials. Tie them in place with crêpe paper or ribbon.
✧ Make a collection of red or heart-shaped objects.
✧ Cut hearts out of gift wrap and make patterns.

CARNIVAL / PANCAKE DAY

Objective

Music – To make and play musical instruments.

Group size

Whole group; three / four at a time.

What you need

Selection of decorative materials, thread, metal bottle tops with holes in, large tin, dried peas / rice, tins with lids, lengths of dowel, tin lid with a hole in it, metal spoons, cooling rack or something similar, cardboard tubes, bells, string, paper plates, open boxes, elastic bands, yoghurt pots or paper cups, stapler, adhesive and scissors.

Preparation

Make holes in the metal tops, lids and cardboard rolls.

What to do

Let the children choose what instruments they want to make. Assist them in making the basic instrument but give them the opportunity to individualise their instruments by making simple adjustments and varying the decorations. Choose from these:

Shaker / rattle – thread metal bottle tops and tie both ends.

Shaker tin – add dried peas or rice to a tin with the lid pressed down very firmly.

Yoghurt shaker – as above but with two yoghurt pots or paper cups fixed together.

Paper plate shaker – fold paper plate in half, add a 'dowel' handle and staple around the edge of all except the last few centimetres. Add dried peas and complete the stapling.

Scrapers – rub a spoon across a cooling rack or similar bumpy surface.

Cardboard shaker – tie bottle tops or bells to the top of a tube.

Tambourine – make holes around a paper plate. Tie bottle tops or bells around the plate.

Stringed instruments – place several elastic bands around open boxes, vary the tension to give different sounds.

When all of the instruments are completed choose a happy song that is familiar to all of the children and sing it with an instrumental accompaniment.

Discussion

Talk about the connections between Carnival and Pancake Day. Explain that they are both associated with enjoying yourself before the fasting period of Lent and take place just before Ash Wednesday (February / March). Local customs developed across Europe such as pancake races in Olney and eating pretzels in parts of Germany. One of the most famous celebrations was Carnival that involved flower floats, processions, masks and dancing in the streets. The tradition was taken to some of the Caribbean islands and the Southern States in the United States of America. This eventually led to steel band music and the present day Carnivals.

Talk about the different sounds made by the instruments. How can they be varied by making quite simple adjustments? What decorations would be suitable? Would streamers help to create a Carnival atmosphere? Talk about the local customs associated with Pancake Day. Do the children take part in any of them?

Follow-up activities

✧ Make and eat pancakes. Try different fillings.

✧ Ask families about local customs and get involved in any community activities.

✧ Listen to the music of a steel band.

✧ Hold a fancy dress procession and dance to the music of a steel band. Choose a theme for the costumes such as spots, flowers or butterflies.

✧ Use the photocopiable sheet on page 95 to develop observation skills.

CHAPTER 7 DISPLAYS

Interesting and attractive displays can be used to provide starting points for a topic, to reinforce ongoing learning or as a celebration of a completed project. Four specific display ideas are provided here related to sections of this book.

Ideally any display should be a planned part of your topic work whether it is as part of the introduction or as a conclusion to the activity. A display can also work as a vehicle for informing families about what their children are doing in your group and involving them in any activities.

When you are preparing a multi-faith display make sure that you don't present a stereotyped view or paint an 'exotic' picture. Any religious artefacts which you include should be treated with respect and only touched when hands are clean and an adult is present. Treat children's work with respect and give it equal status to materials which have been purchased or borrowed. By involving children and their families in your displays they are unlikely to remain static!

HARVEST

What you need

Display board and table covered in autumn colours such as brown or orange, (use fabric on the table if possible), paper for labels and leaves, small paper plates, samples of fruit and vegetables, examples (from page 18) of the children's paintings and models of fruit and vegetables, examples of wild berries, acorns, conkers and leaves, paint or crayons.

Preparation

Cover the board and the table. Cut out large letters to spell 'A u t u m n'. Select sufficient of the children's paintings for the size of your board and mount them on paper in an autumnal colour.

What to do

Involve the children in arranging the paintings and prints giving equal status to both. Label them with the names of the artists.

Decorate enough plates to hold the model and real fruit and vegetables and arrange the exhibits on the decorated plates. Ask the children to arrange the plates on the tables and you can label them in a similar way. Arrange the wild berries, acorns, conkers and leaves on the table.

Cut out paper leaf shapes and ask the children to colour them in autumnal shades. Stick these along the edge of the fabric and display board.

Discussion

Discuss the similarities and differences in the exhibits. Remind the children that although different, they are equally valid. Talk about the colours in the display. Why do the children think they are used? Discuss the colours of autumn and why leaves change colour. What is the connection between 'Autumn' and 'Harvest'? Why is Harvest Festival held at that time of year? Talk about the fruits, both cultivated and wild, that are available at this time of year.

RANGOLI

What you need

A dark coloured background sheet, large square sheet of paper, coloured chalks, small pieces of paper in different shapes and colours, adhesive, children's small rangoli patterns (from Chapter 2), selection of small unbreakable mirrors, fabric table covering (plain sari fabric with a border design would be ideal).

Preparation

Fold the large sheet of paper in half and half again so that, when opened out, the sheet is divided into four. Fold along the diagonal to form eight sections. Cover the table with fabric.

What to do

Colour each section using the coloured chalks so that opposite sections are the same colour. Position the small pieces of paper onto the coloured pattern so that they also form a symmetrical pattern. Take care to match shape, colour and size. When complete, fold the sheet of paper along the axis, and cut it to form an interesting shape around the children's patterns. Mount the picture in the centre of the backing sheet.

Write 'Rangoli patterns' in large print as a title and colour either the lettering or the background with coloured chalk. Place this above the pattern. On a second sheet of paper record the children's group descriptions of how it was made. Display the children's own symmetrical patterns on the table, (see page 19). Place the mirrors alongside them along the axis.

Discussion

Talk about the way in which rangoli patterns are used as a welcome in doorways during the Divali festival. Discuss alternative ways to make them using chalk, powder or rice. Discuss symmetry and making patterns the same on both sides of the axis. Look for other examples of symmetry at home or in the street. Experiment with the mirror by drawing simple shapes and examining their reflection in the mirror.

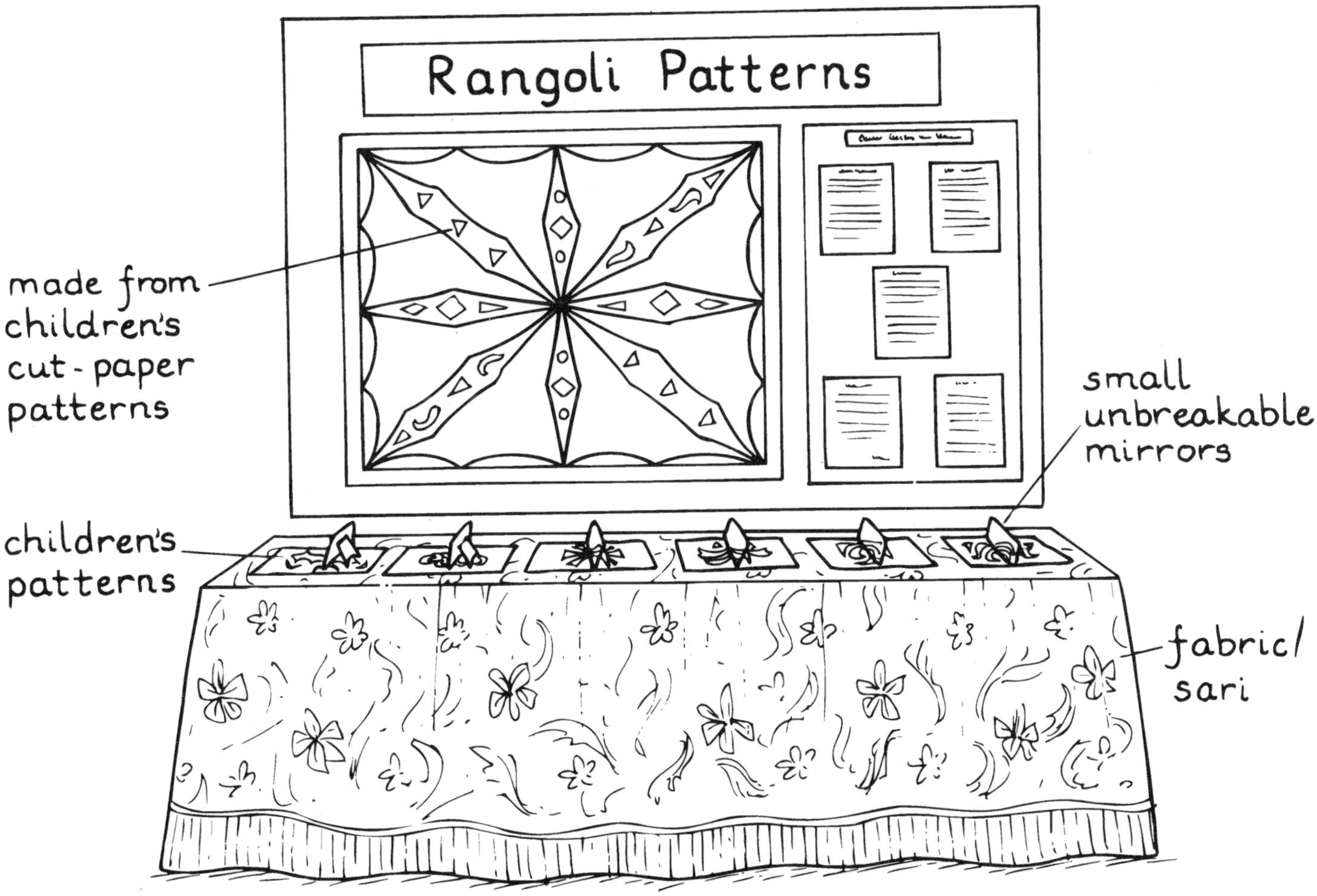

Rangoli Patterns

made from children's cut-paper patterns

small unbreakable mirrors

children's patterns

fabric/sari

CHINESE NEW YEAR

What you need

A display board covered with gold or yellow backing paper, a red border cut with a wavy edge, a table to fit under the display draped in red, yellow or gold fabric (or crêpe paper), items made by the children (from Chapter 5), artefacts loaned by families, paper and pens to make labels, sticky tape or staples, letter to families, paper for double mounting if needed.

Preparation

Cover the table and board with red and gold materials. Send a letter to families explaining that you are planning the display and would like to include contributions from home such as chopsticks, a wok or decorations.

What to do

Explain to the children that you are planning to make a display with their Chinese New Year work. It will include some of the items that they have made together with other things which can be contributed.

Make a selection of things which the children have made such as a banner, card, cut paper work, blossom tree, lucky bag and a story illustration. Try to include the children in making the selection and ensure that all of the work is valued, not just the selected pieces. Make labels for the items and a larger label to explain that the display is a part of the group's Chinese New Year work.

Ask a small group to work with you to arrange the materials. Try to leave spaces for any items that will be added temporarily. Make labels for these as necessary. Some items might look more effective if double mounted. If so, keep to the same colour scheme, for maxiumum effect.

Discussion

Explain that red and gold are the colours traditionally associated with the festival. Streets, shops and homes would be decorated with similar good luck symbols. Discuss ways in which the children decorate their homes for special occasions.

BONFIRE NIGHT

What you need

Display board covered with a dark background, children's 'fireworks' (from page 55) on the same background, strong adhesive, stapler, glitter, dry sticks, fire-coloured tissue, crêpe paper and Cellophane.

Preparation

Select children's artwork (see page 55) to be placed around the bonfire. Involve the children in making a glitter border to the background before it is put into position.

What to do

Make a bonfire by crumpling the paper and fixing it to the background. Attach the sticks to form a bonfire shape. Add individual flames with red paper shapes. Mount the children's work around the bonfire. Make the title using orange or red paper, felt-tipped pens and glitter.

Discussion

There are no spectators in this group picture although, obviously, there would be at a bonfire. Where do the children think they might be? Talk about the need to stay a safe distance from a fire and all the safety aspects of Bonfire Night. Talk about the sights and sounds associated with a bonfire and fireworks. How do they make the children feel? Encourage the use of descriptive language to express their ideas.

Bonfire night

Joe

Sue

Robert

Su

children's artwork

Sarah

Judith

Kerrie

Joshua

We used paint and glitter to make our pictures sparkle!

Ben

sticks

red paper shapes

Helen

Ellie

crumpled paper

CHAPTER 8 ASSEMBLIES

Opportunities for group sharing times and assemblies abound with any celebration of festivals. Harvest, festivals of light and birthdays provide themes for the three specific assembly plans provided here.

HARVEST THANKSGIVING

In the assembly children can draw on experiences they may have had during practical activities on this topic. Throughout the topic work they should have also been encouraged to become aware of how fortunate they are to have such a varied and plentiful supply of food, while others in the world are often hungry. Charities, such as Christian Aid, CAFOD and Oxfam produce useful materials for schools which focus on this and other related issues (see page 96 for addresses).

The assembly can lay the foundations for a future understanding of how bread is used as a symbol of community in a variety of religious traditions, especially Christianity.

Introduction

Play appropriate recorded music such as 'Harvest for the World' by the Isley Brothers or The Christians whilst the children enter for your assembly or group sharing times to highlight the themes of this particular gathering. Alternatively, a traditional hymn, such as 'I am the Bread of Life' could be played or sung.

Begin by encouraging the children to recall as many different types of bread as possible; these could be listed on a flip chart or recorded in other ways – children could display appropriate labels with pictures or models they have made.

Invite the children to present any other relevant work which they have done to the group. This might include songs, poems and rhymes all about breads of various kinds.

Summarise this introduction by ensuring that the children have understood that bread occurs in many different forms throughout the world and is an essential part of most diets.

Activity

Invite a representative of each class or group to come into the centre of the gathering and place a different kind of bread on a low table where everyone can see it. The selection might include a baguette, a pitta bread, a naan, rye bread, soda bread and a ciabatta; these breads could have been made or at least contributed by the children concerned.

When all the breads have been put on the table, surround them with some little candles or night lights and invite the children to spend a few silent moments in looking at the display, focusing on one particular kind of bread.

Ask the children to close their eyes and to think about everything that happened to bring that loaf into being. Encourage them to reflect on relevant work they have done in the past, the visits they may have made to the farm, the bakery or the supermarket and the actual process of making and cooking the loaf which they have brought to contribute to the display.

Reflection

Break up each of the different types of bread and put the pieces into a basket which can be passed around to all the children present. Ask the children to notice everything they can about the piece of bread which they are holding in their hands – its appearance, its smell, its texture. Before they actually taste their portion of bread, encourage them to reflect on all that has made it possible for them to eat and enjoy it.

Prayer

Some children may wish to thank God for the bread which is essential in their lives and pray for those who are deprived of it.

It may also be appropriate to use a traditional prayer at this point, though it may be necessary to simplify the language used. Suitable examples could include the Lord's Prayer from the Christian tradition or a Jewish blessing from the celebration of Shabbat.

Song

A recording of a popular song such as 'Feed the World', by Band Aid could be played as the children leave the gathering. Alternatively, Ready for Harvest on page 75 would be suitable.

FESTIVALS OF LIGHT

This assembly provides the opportunity for children to explore some of the many different ways in which light features in their own lives. They will be able to draw on experiences they have had during other activities, particularly in science, design and technology and language work which will all have contributed to their understanding of the many different ways in which light is used in the world around them.

The assembly should help children to understand the way in which light is used as a symbol in festivals from a variety of faith traditions.

Introduction

Begin by inviting the children to explore and identify how, why and when light is used in a range of situations.

They could illustrate their examples by showing paintings, drawings, collages or models or by performing simple mimes, dramas or role-plays depicting street lights, traffic lights, fairy lights, lighthouses, torches and candles on a birthday cake.

Now invite the children to give reasons for the use of these different light sources – some are linked with safety in the darkness, while others may be featured to mark special occasions. In a small group, it may be possible to encourage spontaneous responses from individual children, but in a larger gathering some preparation may be necessary.

Activity

Sit the children in a circle, gradually close the curtains and blinds in the room, and if facilities allow, slowly dim the lights until the area is as dark as possible.

After a short while, illuminate some candles in the centre of the circle. These should be of different colours, shapes and sizes and could also include both scented and floating candles. It may be appropriate to feature types of candles which are connected with particular religious festivals, such as Advent candles, an Advent ring, Christingles, divas and hanukiahs. Some, or all of these could have been designed and made by the children themselves.

Reflection

In silence, invite the children to think about how they felt at each stage of the exercise and to describe their feelings as they sat in the darkness and then in the light of the candles. You could accompany the reflection with a recording of appropriate music playing quietly in the background.

Some children may be willing to share their thoughts with the rest of the group and these responses could be recorded later as part of a light and dark wall display.

Prayer

Many traditional prayers link with the themes of darkness and light and the religious festivals which draw on those themes. It may therefore be appropriate to select one which relates to a particular celebration.

Children may prefer to say their own prayers, thanking God for the gifts of light and darkness – either offered spontaneously or prepared in advance.

Song

'This little light of mine' is a simple song which would work well within this context and could be sung by some of the children present. Other songs, which have specific links with one or more of the festivals featured, could be chosen from the selection on pages 76 and 77 in this book.

NB Take adequate safety precautions when using any form of naked light with children. When embarking on any discussion on the symbolism associated with darkness and light, remember the positive and negative aspects of both.

Encourage the children to think about the ways in which birthday celebrationsallow us to show our love or friendship for those people who are important to us.

BIRTHDAYS

This approach gives an opportunity to look at birthdays and the way in which they indicate the special regard in which a person may be held.

Before the assembly, make sure the children have been given a wide range of opportunities to develop their awareness of different kinds of birthday celebrations. There might be occasions when they focus on birthdays in school or in their playgroup by bringing sweets or cakes to share with their peers, by lighting birthday candles or singing birthday songs. Many stories, songs, poems and rhymes feature birthdays and these would give the children further insight into how we celebrate birthdays.

The assembly should help children to appreciate the nature of celebration and will help them to develop an understanding of how birthdays give us an opportunity to show how and why we consider some people to be special.

Introduction

Begin by inviting the children to share any relevant work with one another – songs can be sung, poems and rhymes can be recited and pictures, posters, models and charts or graphs can be displayed.

Read a simple story with a birthday theme to the gathering or let some of the children act it out. *Spot's Birthday* by Eric Hill (Heinemann) would be suitable.

Activity

Set out a large table ready for an imaginary birthday tea with a cake, candles, cards, presents, balloons and a 'Happy Birthday' banner. Ask the children to identify all the things they can see which indicate that this is a special celebration.

Invite some of the children in the audience to participate in some traditional birthday party games, such as 'pass the parcel' or 'musical statues'.

Reflection

Ask the children to spend a few quiet moments in thinking about their own birthday celebrations – the people who shared those happy times with them, the cards, presents and good wishes they received and the feelings they experienced.

Invite the children to think of ways in which they could help to make birthdays special times for the people who are important to them. Some children may be willing to share their ideas with the other children.

Prayer

End the gathering by encouraging the children to think of the ways in which Christians may celebrate the birthday of Jesus or Sikhs celebrate the birthday of Guru Nanak and show them some relevant pictures and artefacts. Emphasise the elements of those celebrations – such as the giving and receiving of cards – which will be familiar to them from their own experiences.

Song

'Happy Birthday' is the obvious choice for a song, but consider Christmas carols or a song about Guru Nanak which would also be appropriate.

Collective worship in schools

The assemblies outlined here are suitable for use with children in nurseries and playgroups, but would need to be adapted for use with pupils at registered schools. As a result of legislation enacted in 1944, 1988 and 1993, there are now specific points to be observed when developing a programme of Collective Acts of Worship in a school.

Further guidance will be available from your local SACRE – Standing Advisory Council for RE.

POEMS AND ACTION RHYMES

HARVEST TIME

Harvest time,
Harvest time,
Flowers,
Fruit
And
Grain.

Seeds were sown,
Crops have grown
In sunshine,
Wind
And
Rain.

Wes Magee

HARVEST FESTIVAL

H is for harvest
from flour we make bread.
A is for apples
all rosy and red.
R is for runners
the beans that grow tall.
V is for vegetables
We eat them all.
E is for eggs
Some big and some small.
S is for sunshine –
to ripen the wheat.
T is for thanksgiving,
for food that we eat.

Jan Pollard

SEASIDE HARVEST

Up the creek and into the town,
Our nets are in and our sails are down.
We're bringing home the harvest of the sea.

First there's the blessing of the boats
Then a parade with bands and floats
And back for a feast of fish upon the quay!

Sue Cowling

DIVALI

Ravana's gone,
the demon king has done!
Now once again
with feasting and with prayer
we light a thousand guiding lamps
to welcome Rama here
and bring good fortune
for the coming year.

Judith Nicholls

DIVALI STARTS TODAY

Putting oil lamps round the door,
Making patterns on the floor,
Sending cards to all our friends,
Happy that the monsoon ends.

Giving fruit and sticky sweets,
Lighting fireworks in the streets.
In the temple we all pray,
Now Divali starts today!

Wendy Larmont

IT'S CHRISTMAS TIME!

Carols drift across the night.
Holly gleams by candlelight.
Roaring fire, a spooky tale.
Ice and snow and wind and hail.
Santa seen in High Street store.
Television...more and *more.*
Mince pies, turkey, glass of wine.
Acting your own pantomime.
Socks hung up. It's Christmas time!

Wes Magee

HANUKKAH

When three stars have come out
The first candle can be lit.
Place the lamp on the windowsill
Where we can all see it!
Play a game with a spinning top
And remember deeds of old.
Eat your potato pancakes up
Before they grow cold!

Sue Cowling

CHRISTMAS EVE

Nearly midnight;
still can't sleep!
Has he been yet?
Dare I peep?

Sneak out softly,
creaking floor!
Down the stairs
and through the door...
In the darkness
by the tree,
tightly wrapped...
but which for me?
Feel the ribbon,
find the card!
This one? That one?
Heart thumps hard.
Trembling fingers,
throbbing head,
then...

a voice yells

'BACK TO BED!'

Judith Nicholls

CHINESE LION DANCE

Moving along with many feet
the lion dances up the street.
Humping his back and shaking his head,
opening his mouth, with tongue of red,
moving fowards, writhing, turning,
enormous eyes, gleaming, burning,
as the rhythm drives him on
until the lion dance is done.

Rhythm: use drums, bells and shakers as the lion dances.

Movement: children form a long line, making the body of the lion, holding onto the waist of the child in front, with their heads down. Starting off on the same foot and moving in rhythm to the music, the line should twist and turn as the children follow the movements of the leader.

Child in front should wear a Chinese Lion mask and dictate the movement of the line. (The Chinese Lion looks the same as the Chinese Dragon.)

Jan Pollard

A NEW BABY AT CHRISTMAS

What would *you* give a
baby for Christmas?
A baby who'd just been born.
Would you give him a toy to play with,
or something to keep him warm?
Do you think you would take
a new born lamb,
or frankincense, myrrh or gold?
Like the shepherds who went to see Jesus,
and the kings, in the story of old.

So what would *you* give
a baby for Christmas?
The most precious gift of all.
A welcome with loving kindness,
with happiness and with joy.
For once, in a stable long ago,
there was born, a baby boy.

Jan Pollard

SUKKOT

Myrtle, palm and willow;
willow, myrtle, palm.

Wave your branches to the earth,
raise them to the sun.

Myrtle, palm and willow;
willow, myrtle, palm.

Stretch your branches north and west,
swing them all around.

Myrtle, palm and willow;
willow, myrtle, palm.

Spread your branches south and east,
swing them all around.

Myrtle, palm and willow;
willow, myrtle, palm.

Swing your branches to the earth,
wave them all around;
show that God is everywhere,
raise them to the sun!

Myrtle, palm and willow;
willow, myrtle, palm.

Judith Nicholls

CARNIVAL TIME

Sing me a song.
Tell me a rhyme.
Dance me a dance.
It's Carnival Time.

Put on a costume.
Paint your face.
Beat those drums
all over the place.

Tell all the girls.
Tell all the boys.
Today is the day
for colour and noise.

Sing me a song.
Tell me a rhyme.
Dance me a dance.
It's Carnival Time.

Tony Mitton

GURU NANAK'S BIRTHDAY

Today is very special.
It's full moon day, today.
We're going to the temple
To worship and to pray.

We'll listen to the stories
And share the festive food.
Everyone's excited
And in a happy mood.

Today is very special.
It's full moon day, today.
Today we're celebrating
Guru Nanak's Birthday.

John Foster

PANCAKES

Pancakes, pancakes,
one by one.
Toss them, catch them,
just for fun.

Pancakes, pancakes,
two by two.
One for me
and one for you.

Pancakes, pancakes,
three by three.
Pancakes, piled up
for my tea.

Pancakes, pancakes,
four by four.
Eat them up
and make some more.

Pancakes tossed up
in the air...
Whoops! There's pancake
in my hair!

(This can be an action rhyme, with simple mime)

Tony Mitton

FIREWORKS

(A chant for two groups of voices)
Squibs and sparklers
Squibs and sparklers

Golden showers
Golden showers

Shooting stars and Catherine wheels
Shooting stars and Catherine wheels

Fiery flowers
Fiery flowers

Racing rockets
Racing rockets

Flashing fountains
Flashing fountains

Whirling windmills
Whirling windmills

Blazing mountains
Blazing mountains

Light the paper...

Watch them whizzing

Watch them whizzing

Watch them whizzing

BANG!

Judith Nicholls

ON BONFIRE NIGHT

On Bonfire Night,
On Bonfire Night,
Guy Fawkes
wears old boots.

On Bonfire Night,
On Bonfire Night,
a giant rocket
shoots.

On Bonfire Night,
On Bonfire Night,
sparks are flying
high.

On Bonfire Night,
On Bonfire Night,
new stars light up
the sky.

Wes Magee

VALENTINE CARD

Make it with sequins, pretty lace or glitter
Make it with paper, lentils or litter
Make it with crayons, red paint or ink
Colour it bright scarlet, crimson or pink...
Make it say you love me, make it just to tease...
But make me a valentine, please, please, please!

Geraldine Taylor

GRANDPA'S DAY

It's Grandpa's Day tomorrow
I've made him a lovely card.
Mum helped me with all of the colours.
We both worked really hard.

We went to the shop to buy one
But we didn't like what we saw.
The shop-lady said she was sorry,
She didn't have any more.

You see – all the cards showed Grandpas
As old and wrinkly and slow.
But my Grandpa's fun and ever so young.
I know – he told me so!

Margaret Eustace

NEW YEAR

This night
of all the nights
is the year's last.
All, all
the other nights
are gone, are past...

After
the evening, with
its fading light,
put the lid
on the hour
and close it tight.

Close up
your tired eye,
close up the day.
Bid the old year
Goodbye,
and come away.

Jean Kenward

LIGHT THE FESTIVE CANDLES

(for Hanukkah)
Light the first of eight tonight –
the farthest candle to the right.

Light, the first and second, too,
when tomorrow's day is through.

Then light three, and then light four –
every dusk one candle more.

Till all eight burn bright and high,
honouring a day gone by

When the Temple was restored,
rescued from the Syrian lord,

and an eight-day feast proclaimed –
The Festival of Lights – well named

To celebrate the joyous day
when we regained the right to pray
to our one God in our own way.

Aileen Fisher

CARNIVAL FOR MARDI GRAS

(A steel band recording will add to the rhythm and atmosphere)

Everyone:
We're going to dance in the carnival,
for Mardi Gras.

Ist Child:
I shall be a peacock and
spread my tail out wide.
Looking like a rainbow,
Twirling like a top,
and I'm never, never, never
never, NEVER going to stop!

Chorus:
(chanted by whole group, to steel band music)
We'll dance in the morning,
and we'll dance in the night,
and we'll dance through the darkness
until it is light.

2nd Child:
I shall be a butterfly,
with wings of white and yellow.
Looking like a rainbow,
Twirling like a top,
and I'm never, never, never
never, NEVER going to stop!

Chorus: (as before)

3rd Child:
I shall be a bumblebee,
dressed in gold and black.
Looking like a rainbow,
Twirling like a top,
and I'm never, never, never
never, NEVER going to stop!

Chorus: (as before)

4th Child:
I shall be a parrot,
with wings of blue and red.
Looking like a rainbow,
Twirling like a top,
and I'm never, never, never
never, NEVER going to stop!

Chorus: (as before)

5th Child:
I shall be a hummingbird,
darting to and fro.
Looking like a rainbow,
Twirling like a top,
and I'm never, never, never
never, NEVER going to stop!

Chorus (as before)

6th Child:
I'm a bird of Paradise.
See the feathers in my tail.
Looking like a rainbow,
Twirling like a top,
and I'm never, never, never
never, NEVER going to stop!

Chorus (as before)

*Other colourful characters
can be added in the same style.*

Jan Pollard

SONGS

AUTUMN HARVEST

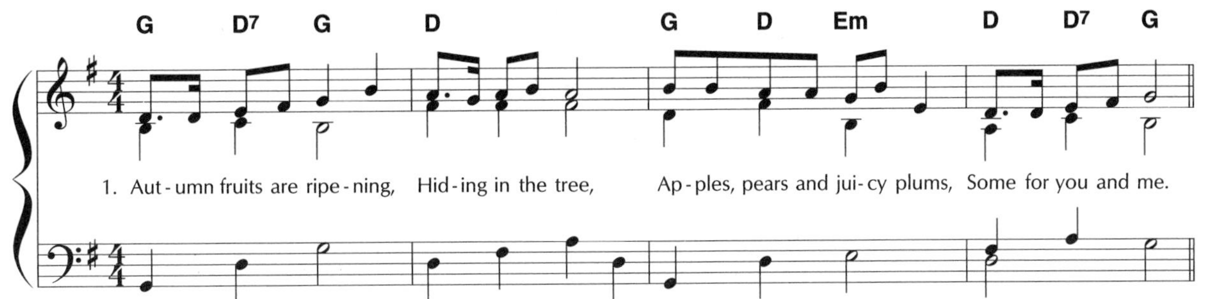

2. Bring a woven basket,
Fill it carefully
With the fruit so ripe and full,
Some for you and me.

3. Apple cake and plum jam,
Cherry tarts for tea,
Blackberries and raspberries too,
Some for you and me.

Jean Gilbert

READY FOR HARVEST

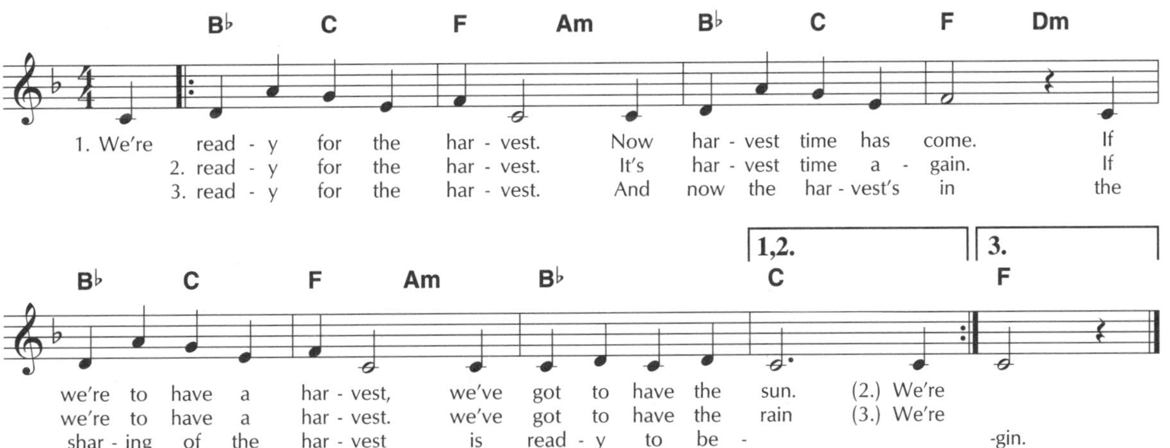

Clive Barnwell

HARVEST ROUND

Tune: London's burning

Jan Holdstock

WELCOME DIVALI

Peter Morrell

CANDLE LIGHT

This song can be used for many multi-faith celebrations. The word 'special' can be changed for 'Christmas' or 'Divali' (if you borrow the note before – i.e. 'Lights up the dark on Divali night.').

One child carrying a candle (or a model candle of card with a tissue paper flame), stands in the centre of the ring while a few voices sing. In verse 2 another candle bearer joins in and a few extra voices sing 'Two little candles...'. This cumulative action grows until you have all the candles needed.

Sue Nicholls

ADVENT CALENDAR SONG

This song is sung each morning during December when the next Advent calendar window is opened.

Sue Nicholls

CHINESE NEW YEAR

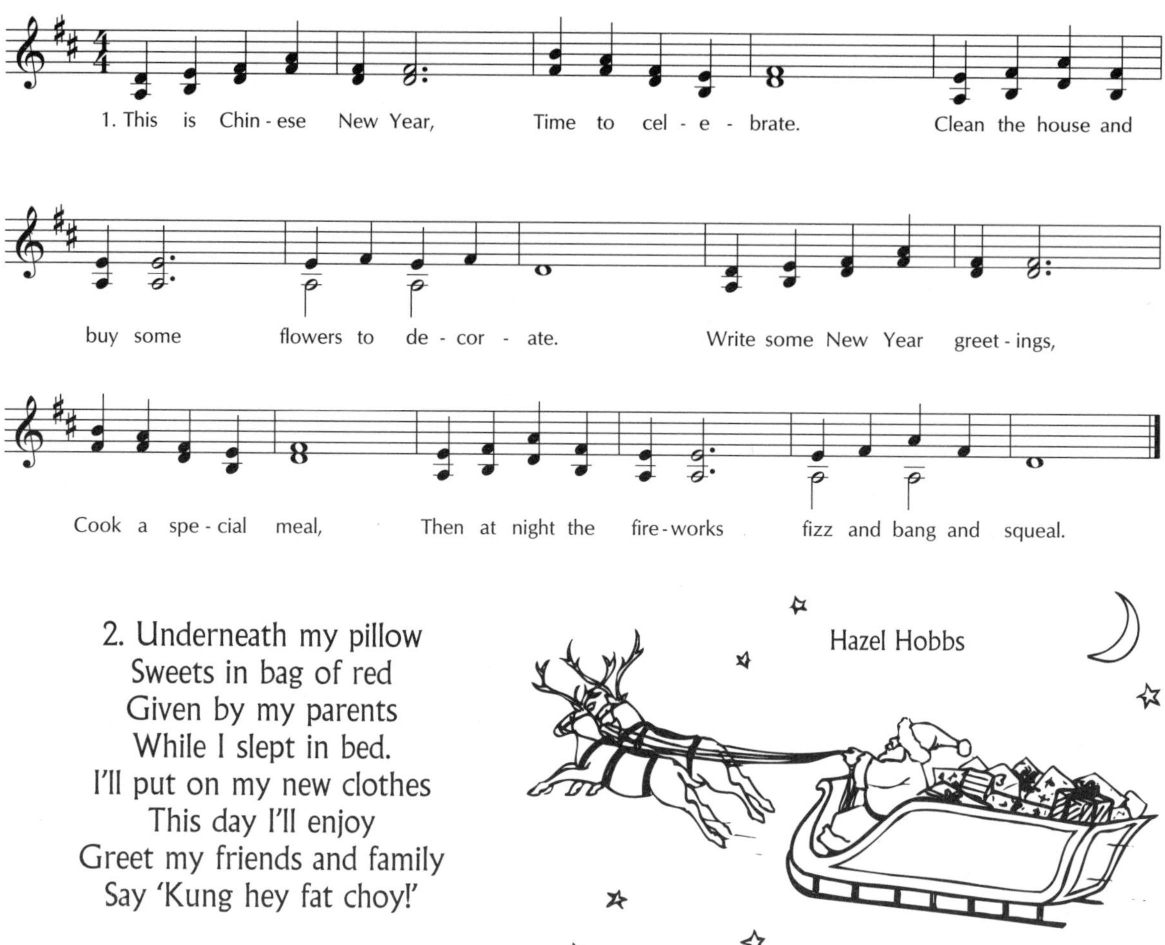

2. Underneath my pillow
Sweets in bag of red
Given by my parents
While I slept in bed.
I'll put on my new clothes
This day I'll enjoy
Greet my friends and family
Say 'Kung hey fat choy!'

Hazel Hobbs

SANTA'S SLEIGH

Tune: Row, row, row your boat

Jan Holdstock

CHRISTMAS

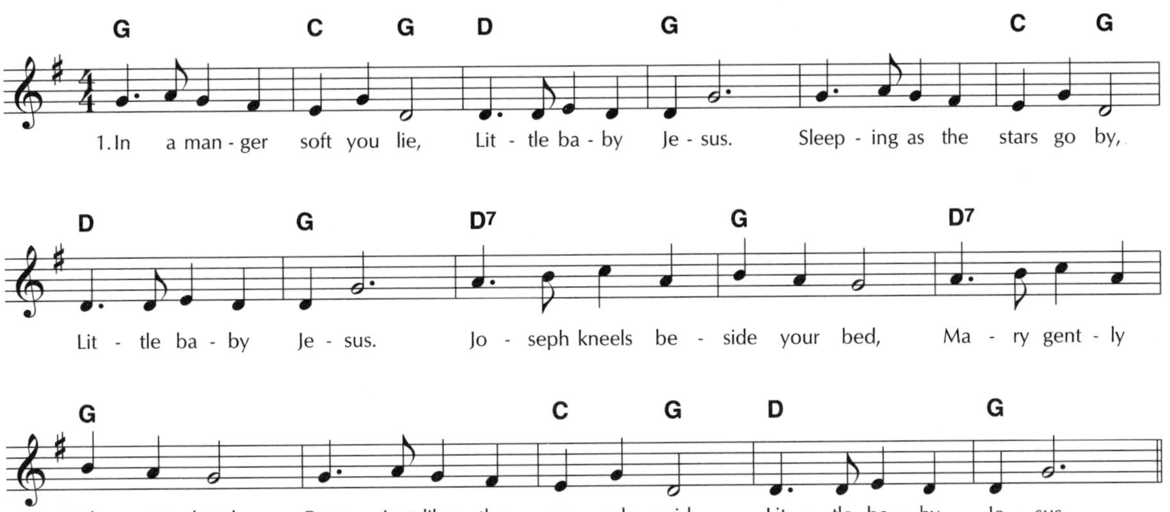

2. As you lie so small and new
Little baby Jesus
Shepherds come and worship you
Little baby Jesus
Wise men from the east draw near
When they see the star appear
Bringing precious gifts to dear
Little baby Jesus.

3. Born two thousand years ago
Little baby Jesus
Through the Bible we can know
Little baby Jesus.
As our presents we undo
Help us to remember too
The best gift of all was you,
Little baby Jesus.

Hazel Hobbs

BONFIRE NIGHT

C G7 C F G7

Whoosh go the rock-ets, green and gold and red, Bang, bang, bang, bang, ex - plod-ing ov-er-head.

C G7 C F G7

Fizz go the fi-re-works, show-er-ing the ground, Whizz go the cath-'rine wheels, whirl-ing round and round. The

Am Dm G7 C F D7 G G7

roar of the fi - re, the crack-le of the flames, see the sil-ver spark - lers hiss-ing out our names.

C G7 C F G7 C

Lis-ten to the air - bombs whee in-to the sky. The sights and sounds of Bon - fire night.

Lesley Funge

STORIES

HANUKKAH
THE FESTIVAL OF LIGHTS

Long, long ago a wicked king marched into the city of Jerusalem with many soldiers. They charged into the streets, set fire to the houses and killed hundreds of people.

Then the soldiers ran into the Temple and stole all the precious holy things that were kept there. Worst of all, they stole the great, seven-branched candlestick, called the menorah, which was kept in front of the altar. For the very first time ever, God's dancing flames, kept alight with a special oil, went out.

The sacred Temple was no longer a place of peace and quiet where the Jewish people could say their prayers and worship God. The soldiers had spoiled it.

The people were very frightened and sad. All except Mattathias *(Mat-a-thy-as)*, who lived in a village outside Jerusalem. He was very angry. 'All your weeping and wailing will not do any good,' he said. 'We will have to fight to get our city and Temple back!'

Mattathias and his five sons, with other brave men who joined them, fought against their enemies for many years, promising not to give up until the candles of the menorah were alight once again in the Temple. Even after Mattathias died, his son Judah carried on the battle until they finally managed to chase the enemy away.

The Jews were free again. They celebrated with dancing and music, then they cleaned the Temple from top to bottom.

But when they came to put back the menorah they found they had only enough holy oil to last one day. So Judah prayed, 'Please, God, let the oil last till we have found some more! We have fought so long and hard. Please do not let the flames go out!'.

God heard his prayer. The flames did not go out. For eight days they burned steadily and brightly. All the Jewish people in the land came to the Temple to see the wonderful flames.

'We must never forget these eight special days,' said Judah. 'From now on, every year at this time, we will always remember them with a joyful festival of lights.'

Many Jewish families keep that promise today. They put a special candlestick on a table, or in a window, and for eight nights they light the candles one by one until all of them are burning brightly. They give thanks to God for that great miracle in the Temple of Jerusalem so long ago.

Jackie Andrews

THE STORY OF DIVALI
FESTIVAL OF LIGHTS

Divali is a joyful festival celebrated by both Hindus and Sikhs. The Hindu version celebrates the story of Rama and Sita and their return to their home after fourteen years of exile in the jungles.

Rama was a prince. He had a favourite brother called Lakshman whom he loved very much. They were good friends and loved to go hunting together with their golden bows and arrows.

Now a king from another part of the country was looking for a husband for his beautiful daughter Sita. He had a special, heavy bow which was very hard to bend, so he sent a message to all the princes that whoever could bend this great bow would be able to marry Sita.

Many princes tried, but no one else could even lift it! When it was Rama's turn, however, he lifted the bow easily and bent it so much it snapped in two.

Rama and Sita were married. The old king wanted Rama to be the next king, but the queen would not hear of it. She wanted her own son to rule. Because the king loved his wife and wanted to please her, he arranged for Rama and Sita to be sent far away, to live in a land of thick jungle. Lakshman went with them.

The three of them lived simply and happily in their jungle home for many years. But far away a wicked demon with ten heads, called Ravana, heard about Sita's beauty and wanted to steal her from Rama. He tricked Sita away from the safety of her home and took her to his palace.

Rama and Lakshman searched for Sita for many days and nights. Then Hanuman, a monkey god, offered to help them. He could travel very fast, over the treetops, and saw Sita in the garden of Ravana's palace. Hanuman gave Sita a ring from Rama and told her she would soon be rescued.

With the monkeys of Hanuman's army beside them, Rama and Lakshman fought a long and terrible battle with Ravana and his demons. The monkeys made a bridge of stones so that the two princes could reach the demon's island. Finally, Rama took a magic arrow – given to him by the sun god, Indira – and shot it straight into Ravana's wicked heart. At last the monster was killed.

It was time for Rama to return home with Sita.

While Rama had been away his father had died, so the people were very happy when the young prince returned to them. He was crowned King with Sita beside him.

All the streets were decorated, there were beautiful fireworks and every house was lit with tiny lamps, making the whole city look like a fairyland.

All this happened a long, long time ago. Today, Hindus celebrate the festival of Divali every winter. They light their homes with little pottery lamps – called *diva* – and fairy lights. They have special food and new clothes and give each other gifts. It is a very happy occasion.

Pronunciation guide	
Sita	*See-tah*
Lakshman	*Luksh-mun*
Ravana	*Rah-vun*
Hanuman	*Han-u-mahn*
Diva	*Thee-yah*
Divali	*Thee-vah-lee*

Susheila Stone

(Abridged from the original)

THE STORY OF DIVALI AS CELEBRATED BY SIKHS

Divali is a winter and religious festival celebrated by both Hindus and Sikhs. The founder of the Sikh religion is Guru Nanak. A guru is a teacher. Nine other Gurus carried on the work of Guru Nanak and there are various festivals through the year to celebrate their anniversaries.

Guru Hargobind was the sixth Guru. He became such a powerful, popular leader of the Sikhs, that even Muslims started to follow him. The Mogul Emperor at the time was not pleased with this. He had Guru Hargobind arrested and thrown into prison, along with fifty-two other Hindu princes.

Two years later the Guru was released, but he refused to leave the prison unless the other Hindus were allowed to go with him. The Emperor said that only those who could hold on to the Guru's clothing as he walked through a narrow passageway would be set free.

Guru Hargobind had a special cloak made for himself, with long tassels. The princes were all able to hold on to these as the Guru walked through the passageway, so they were all freed.

As Guru Hargobind returned home, his path was lit with candles to welcome him.

To remember this day, Sikhs celebrate Divali with lights and fireworks and many visit the *gurdwara* (temple).

Pronunciation guide	
Guru Nanak	*Goo-roo Na-nak*
Guru Hargobind	*Goo-roo Har-go-vind (rhymes with wind)*
gurdwara	*gooth-wah-rah*

Adapted by Jackie Andrews from *Festivals – Teacher Timesavers* (Scholastic).

THE CHINESE NEW YEAR STORY

There were only a few days to New Year and twelve of the animals were arguing. Each animal wanted the new year named after himself. What a noise they made! Roaring, crowing, bleating, hissing, barking and squeaking. They soon woke the gods, who appeared in the sky and asked what was going on. All the animals answered at once.

'Be quiet!' ordered the gods. 'You are all very rude!'

The animals went quiet. One by one they explained why they were arguing and why each felt the new year should be named after them.

The gods listened to them and thought very hard about their problem. They finally decided it would be best to hold a race.

'Can you see the big river?' the gods asked. 'You must all swim across it, and we will name the new year after the one who reaches the other side first.'

The animals all agreed to take part. Secretly, each thought they would win. They lined up along the bank and the gods started them off.

'Ready, steady GO!' they shouted.

There was an enormous splash as the twelve animals leaped into the water. Ox was the strongest swimmer and he soon began to take the lead. When Rat saw this, he cleverly grabbed Ox's tail and climbed onto his back without Ox noticing. As Ox waded the last few steps to the bank, Rat leaped over his head and onto the shore.

'I've won! I've won!' he squeaked.

Ox was very surprised. He had no idea that Rat had cheated.

So the gods named the new year after Rat.

'Next year will be the year of the Ox, because he was second,' they said.

One by one the other animals reached the other side of the river; Tiger, Hare, Dragon, Snake, Horse, Ram, Monkey, Cockerel, Dog and then Pig, who came last.

'You have all done very well,' said the gods, 'so we will name a year after each one of you, in the same order that you finished the race.'

The animals were very tired, but pleased that it was all settled and they didn't have to argue any more!

Jackie Andrews

THE HARVEST FESTIVAL

Now, Simon, can you tell us what we all have to bring to school tomorrow?' asked Mrs Greenway.

Simon frowned as he looked up at his teacher. She'd been talking about the harvest festival tomorrow but he couldn't remember exactly what she'd been saying.

'Food?' he suggested, hopefully.

'That's right,' said Mrs Greenway. 'Tomorrow you all have to bring some food. And after our special harvest assembly, we're going to take the food to local senior citizens.'

Simon was worried about the harvest festival. He was sure he was going to forget something. He had only been at school a few weeks and he found it hard to remember everything. What if he forgot to bring his food, or forgot the words of the special harvest hymns? And what were senior citizens like? They sounded very posh. It was all very worrying.

Mum was waiting for him at the school gates.

'It's harvest day tomorrow,' Simon told her in a rush in case he forgot.

'I know,' smiled Mum. 'And Grandad said we could have some fresh vegetables from his garden. We're going round to see him right now so you can pick some. Would you like that?'

Simon smiled. 'You bet!' He loved visiting Grandad.

Grandad gave Simon a plastic carrier bag. 'Now you fill this up with whatever you like for your harvest festival tomorrow.'

'Thanks, Grandad,' said Simon. He picked some carrots, beans and a big green cabbage. Soon the bag was bulging. Simon took it to the kitchen, where Mum and Grandad were having a cup of tea.

'What are senior citizens like?' he asked them.

'Goodness, what a question!' said Mum. 'Why are you asking that?'

'Because we have to take our food to them tomorrow and I don't know where they live or what they look like!' said Simon .

'Bless my soul!' laughed Grandad. 'Senior citizens are just elderly people like me.'

Simon was glad about that. But he still felt a bit nervous about his first harvest festival.

The next day, Mum helped Simon take the big bag of vegetables to school. She took them into the hall where a special display was being arranged. When Simon went in later for the assembly, he was sure he saw Grandad's cabbage right at the front.

During the thanksgiving service, they sang the special harvest hymns: *All Things Bright and Beautiful* and *We Sow the Fields and Scatter*. Mrs Greenway sang with them, to help them remember the words.

After break, it was time to deliver their decorated shoeboxes full of food. Mrs Greenway went too, and so did three of the mums, so there was no need for Simon to worry about getting lost.

But he was still very nervous, especially when he saw that he and Mandy were the first in line and had to visit the first senior citizen. He felt his knees wobbling as he followed Mrs Greenway down the road. He was so worried, he didn't notice where they were going.

'Right, Simon and Mandy. Let's go and knock on the door,' said Mrs Greenway.

And Simon was halfway down the path before he realised. This was Grandad's house!

Mrs Greenway rang the bell.

Grandad opened the door. 'Hello,' he said. 'What have we here?'

Simon and Mandy handed him the shoebox of food.

'It's a harvest gift for you,' said Simon.

Grandad looked down at the box of food and smiled. 'My word,' he said, '*someone's* grown some fine vegetables. Just look at that cabbage!' He winked at Simon. 'How lovely. Thank you all very much!'

Simon grinned. He was glad Grandad was *his* senior citizen – even if he did have his own cabbage back!

Karen King

Harvest cards

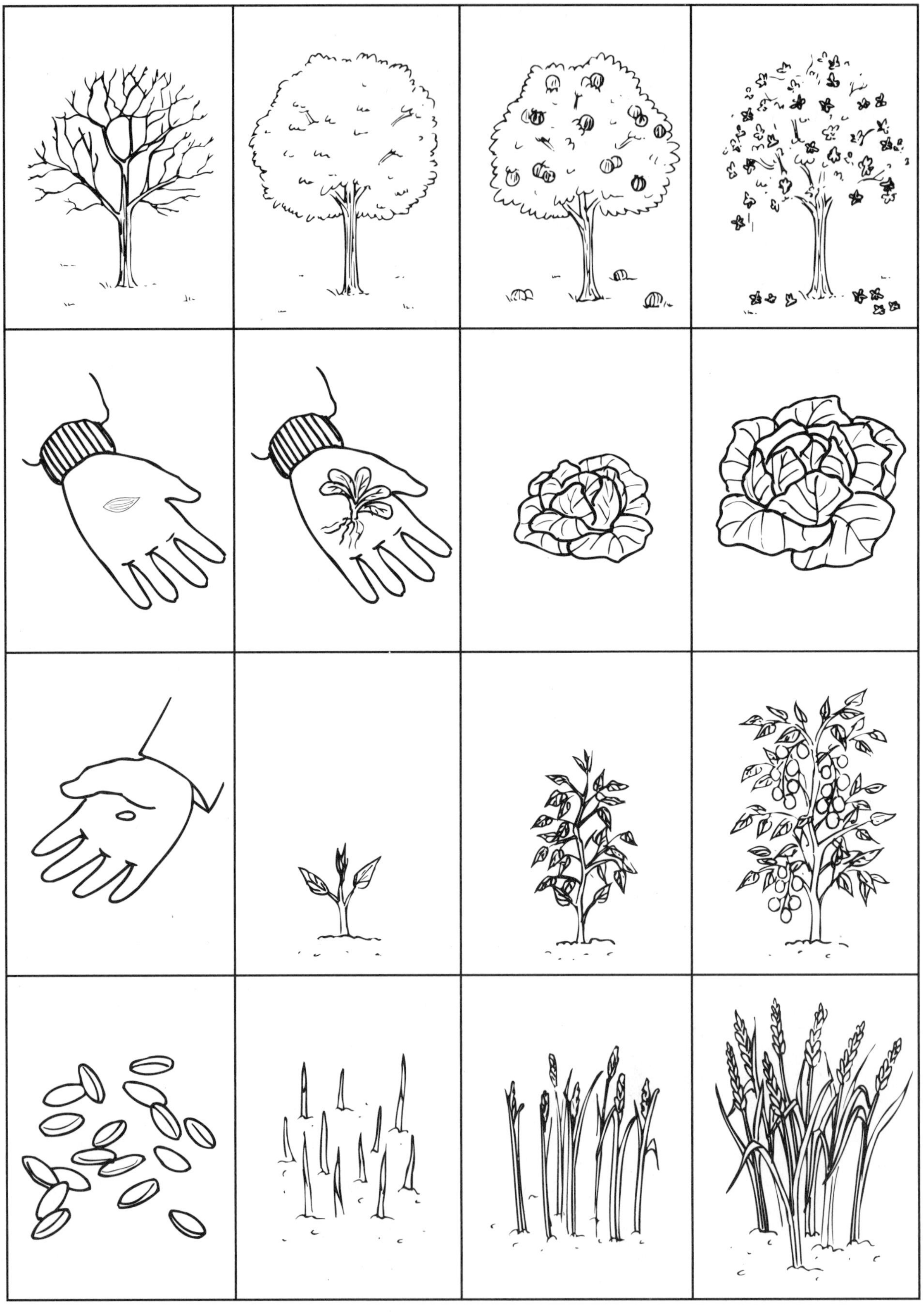

Pretty patterns

- Colour in these Rangoli patterns.

Add a flame

- Add a flame every day.

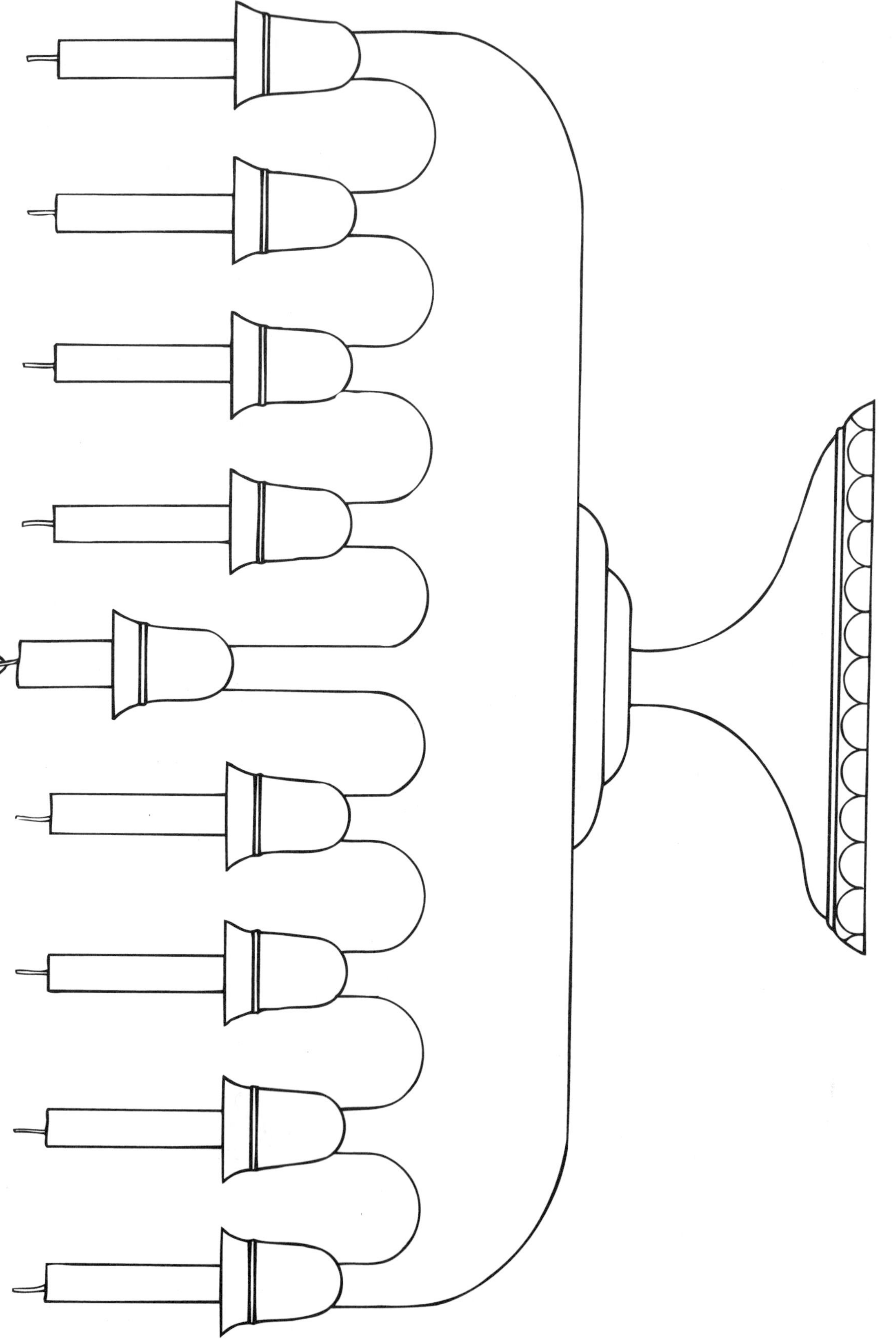

Dreidel board

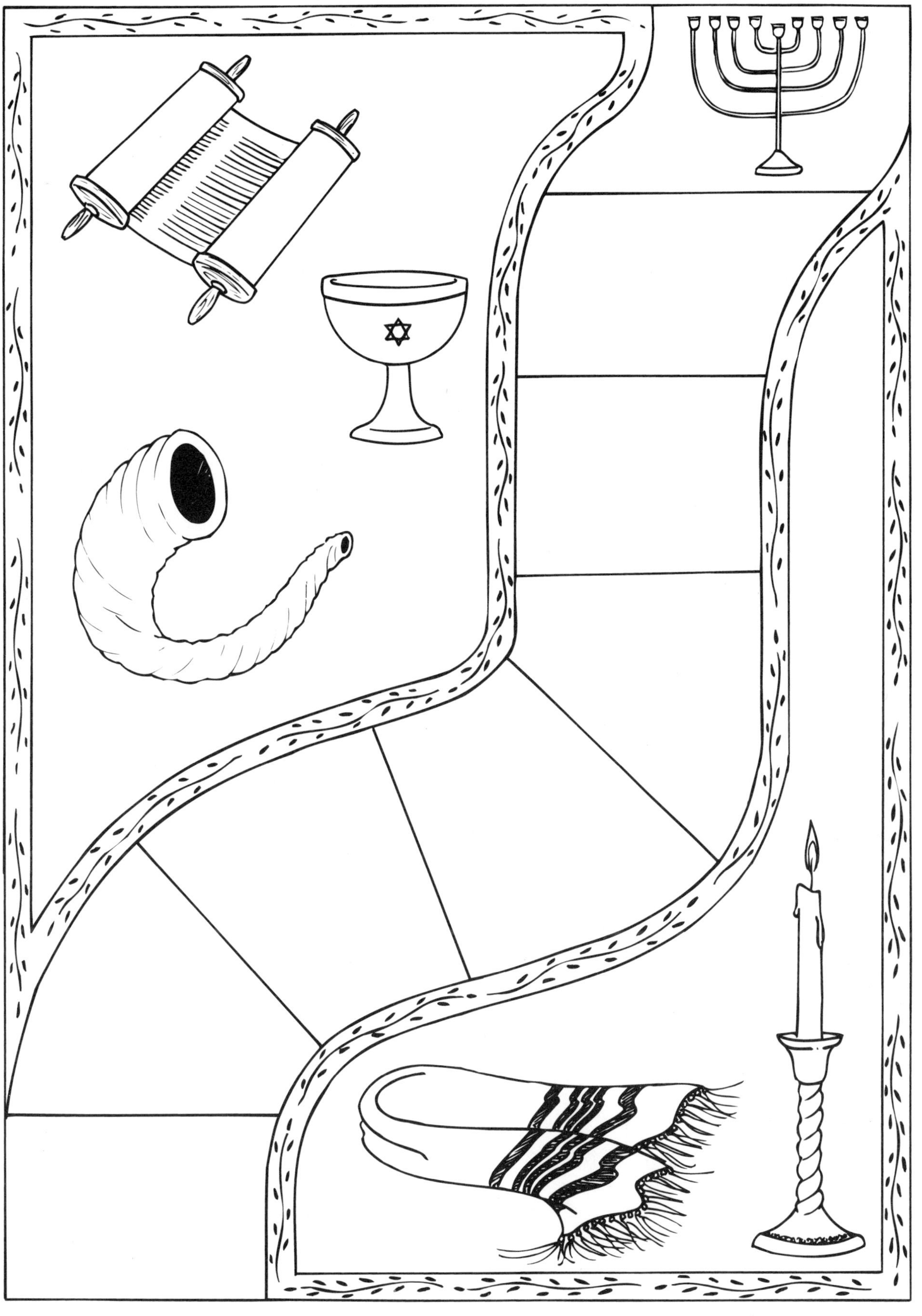

Making patterns

- Use red, green and yellow to colour with repeating patterns

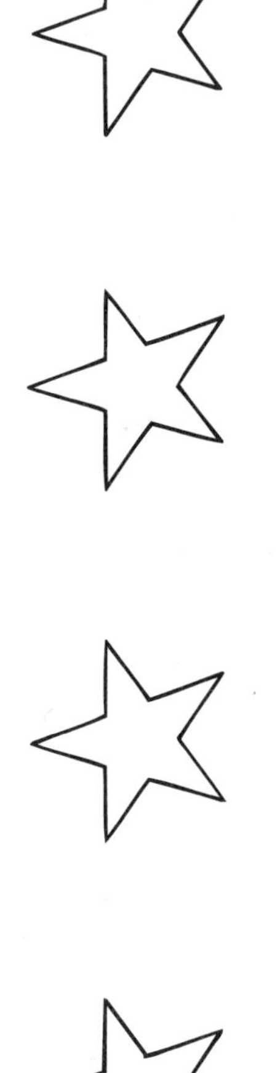

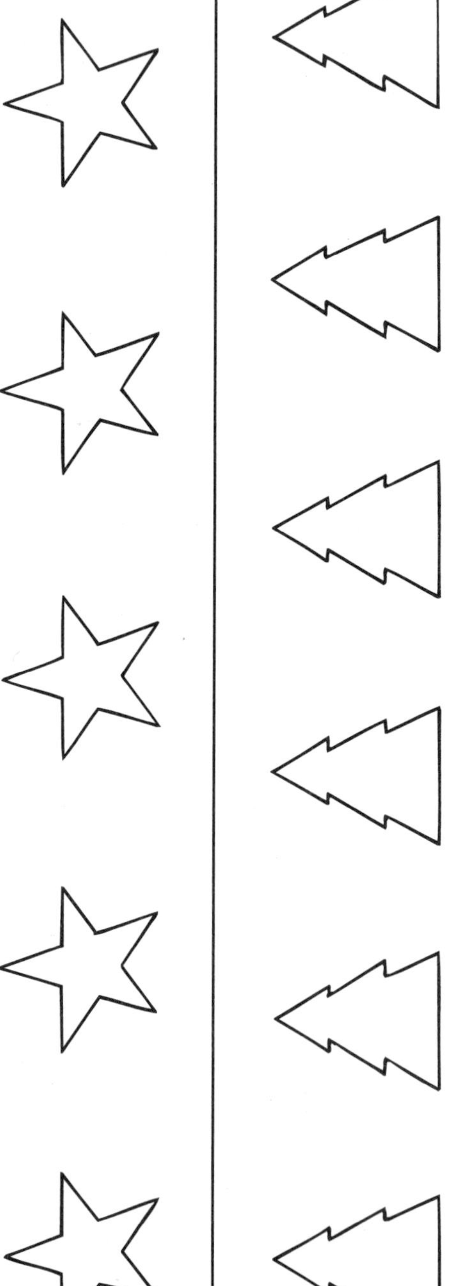

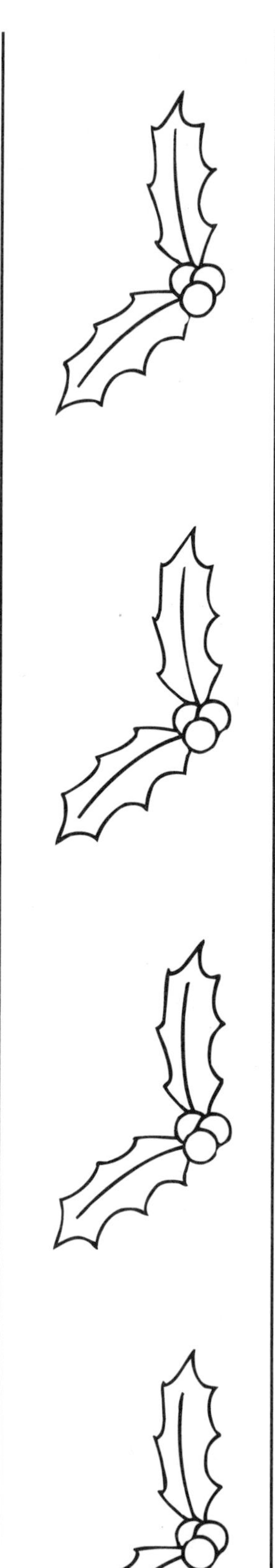

Baby Jesus

- Cut out the pictures and stick them in the right order.

Tails and feathers

Monkey	Dragon	Snake
Ox	Rat	Rabbit
Tiger	Dog	Horse
Pig	Ram	Cockerel

Spot the difference

- Find the differences between these pictures.

RECOMMENDED MATERIALS

STORY BOOKS

The Good Little Christmas Tree Ursula Moray Williams (Walker Books)
Celebration Song James Berry (Picture Puffin)
The Story of Christmas Jane Ray (Orchard Books)
Lights for Gita Rachna Gilmore (Mantra)
Hanukkah Fun Judy Bastyra (Kingfisher Books)
Doing Christmas Sarah Garland (Picture Puffin)

INFORMATION BOOKS

All About Hanukkah Judye Groner, Madeline Wikler and Rosalyn Schanzer (Kar-Ben Copies)
Harvest Celia Brayfield (Penguin)
Harvest Robert Westall (Metheun Children's Books)
Christopher's Harvest Time Elsa Beskow and Joan Tate (Floris Books)
My Class Series (Watts Books)
Our Culture Series (Watts Books)
Celebrations Series (A & C Black)
Celebrations Series (Wayland)
Chinese Spring Festival Ming Tsow (*Way We Live Series*, Hamish Hamilton)
Learn About Festivals Susan Holdaway and Stephen Milligan (Anglia Young Books)
Sunshine Series (non-fiction) (Heinemann)
Celebrations Chris Deshpande (*Worldwide Crafts Series*, A & C Black)
Autumn Rhoda Nottridge (Let's Celebrate Series, Wayland)

POETRY

Let's Celebrate: Festival Poems, John Foster (ed.) (Oxford University Press)

POSTERS AND OTHER RESOURCES

Festivals and Special Days (ref: P58) and *Celebrations* (ref: A17) poster packs comprising 12 A4 colour pictures and teachers' notes are available from: Philip Green Educational Ltd, 112a Alcester Road, Studley, Warwickshire B80 7NR. (Tel: 01527 854711).
Festival puzzles from NES Arnold Ltd, Ludlow Hill Road, West Bridgford, Nottingham NG2 6HD (Tel: 0115 945 2200).
Some LEA's produce their own resources relating to religious and cultural celebrations.

USEFUL ADDRESSES

Schools and Youth Department, Christian Aid, PO Box 100, London SE1 7RT (0171 620 4444).
CAFOD, 2 Romero Close, Stockwell, London SW9 9TY (Tel: 0171 733 7900).
Oxfam UK and Ireland, 274 Banbury Road, Oxford OX2 7DZ (Tel: 01865 311311). Web site (for teachers and young people) – http:\\www.heinemann.co.uk\oxfam\
Christian Education Movement (CEM), Royal Buildings, Victoria Street, Derby DE1 1GW (Tel: 01332 296655) have a variety of useful materials, based on celebrations (both Christian and non-Christian).
Jewish Education Bureau, 8 Westcombe Avenue Leeds LS8 2BS (Tel: 01132 663613) for Jewish resources.
Religion in Evidence Educational Suppliers, Unit 7, Monk Road Industrial Estate, Alfreton, Derbyshire DE55 7RL (Tel: 01773 830255).
Articles of Faith Educational Suppliers, Resource House, Kay Street, Bury, Lancashire BL9 6BU (Tel: 0161 763 6232)
Minority Group Support Services, Prior Deram Walk, Coventry CV4 8FT (Tel: 01203 717800)